DEDICATION

This book is dedicated to all evangelists,
with the prayer that the Lord of the Harvest
will thrust forth many more of them into the
harvesting of the world for Jesus.

From the Author
This is an extraordinary book. The supernatural in the form of dreams, visions and miracles abounds. The author has not attempted to verify each one of the healing miracles as this would be beyond the scope of this work. However, in almost every miracle recorded, hundreds and in many cases thousands of people witnessed the event.

Photos by
David Beard, Ron Steele, Tony Fredrikson,
Karl Heinz Schablowski, Peter van den Berg,
David Dobson and Rob Birkbeck —
all by kind permission of
Christ for all Nations

REINHARD BONNKE

A Passion for the Gospel

REINHARD BONNKE

A Passion for the Gospel

Colin Whittaker

Kingsway Publications
Eastbourne

Biblical quotations are taken from the
New International Version
© 1973, 1978, 1984 by the International Bible Society.

ISBN 0 86065 773 6

Co-published in South Africa with
SCB Publishers
Cornelis Struik House, 80 McKenzie Street
Cape Town 8001, South Africa.
Reg no 04/02203/06

Cover design by Bookprint Creative Services, Eastbourne,UK.
Origination of photo sections by JC Centre, Cairo, Egypt.
and Veldon Printers Limited, Kidderminster, UK.
Typesetting by Neil Edginton.
for
KINGSWAY PUBLICATIONS LTD
Lottbridge Drove, Eastbourne, East Sussex BN23 6NT

Printed in Great Britain.

CONTENTS

Part Three: Into all the World

Foreword

The story goes that a noted eighteenth-century sceptic was spotted by a friend on the edge of a great crowd listening to George Whitefield. He could not resist the temptation to go over and ask, with the hope of embarrassing him, 'What are you doing here? You don't believe what Whitefield preaches, do you?'

'No,' was the response, 'but he does!'

I have listened many times to Reinhard Bonnke since my first meeting with him in 1979 and have never been left in any doubt that he too, like Whitefield, believes what he preaches.

I first wanted to write this book in 1987 because I sensed that the church was in danger of losing its evangelistic soul. In my own ministry, I firmly believe that the Lord called me to be a pastor, albeit a pastor with a pen. I know I am not an evangelist, but as a pastor and an editor I have tried to 'do the work of an evangelist', in the words of Paul to Timothy (2 Timothy 4:5).

I believe in evangelism and in evangelists — with good reason. I owe my wife, Hazel, to a faithful evangelist. She was nineteen years of age and the first time she heard the gospel preached she responded with tears and was truly converted. Her life was immediately transformed and has stood the test of time — fifty years as a Christian and forty-seven as my wife and colleague in pastoral ministry and Christian work. The evangelist who won her to Christ was Tom Butler, together with a Cliff College team of students from that faithful Methodist stronghold of evangelism. Her father, who had been a sergeant major in the army, gave her new-found faith two weeks. How wrong can you be!

I believe in evangelism because I owe the salvation of my own soul to the faithful ministry of Revd James Edward Eagles, MC, who was the superintendent minister of the Methodist Mission in Rochdale — the Thomas Champness Memorial Hall. Unlike my wife I was brought up to attend church regularly, but it was not until our family moved to Rochdale and I had been five months under the ministry of Mr Eagles, that I committed my life to Christ and, for the first time, knew what it meant to be 'born again' and to enter into salvation through Christ as Saviour and Lord. I was fifteen years of age, and since then have enjoyed a lifetime of proving the faithfulness of the Lord Jesus Christ.

I believe in evangelists because I have experienced the fruits of the ministry in churches I have pastored.

I believe in the ministry of evangelist Reinhard Bonnke because I have carefully observed and followed his ministry for over eighteen years. I judge him to be a true evangelist and a successor to the many worthies with the ministry gift of evangelist as listed in Ephesians chapter 3.

I believe the church urgently needs to revive its dying passion for evangelism. The gospel cannot and must not be changed, but our methods must be updated constantly if we are to communicate Christ to our generation.

Every evangelist is of necessity a product of his times, and in this respect Reinhard Bonnke is no exception. The world-shaking events which shaped his early life have been used by the Master Potter to shape a human vessel fit for the post Second World War era — and on, God willing, into the twenty-first century.

I am indebted to many people for their help in writing this book. I am especially grateful to Reinhard Bonnke for trusting me and opening himself to me and giving me prime time in the midst of his demanding schedule. He gave me unrestricted access to himself and all his team, and freedom to ask all the questions I wanted.

I have observed him from near and far for eighteen years, and have listened to him preach and lecture in a wide variety of events and circumstances. I have also read everything I could find which has been written about him, as well as reading and re-reading everything written by him.

The result I trust is a true picture of the man and not in any way a hagiography, i.e., 'a biography that idealises or idolises its subject' (Collins Dictionary) or a 'biography of a saint, a biography which over-praises its subject' (Chambers Dictionary). Any such idolising would be particularly unacceptable to Reinhard Bonnke himself. Ask any of his team and they will all tell you that he abhors any attempts to project his image.

It has been said that 'the New Birth makes the natural man spiritual, and the spiritual man natural'. Reinhard Bonnke is very natural as well as very spiritual. He takes his evangelism very seriously — but not himself. He laughs very readily, and is never afraid to laugh at himself. The many hours I spent interviewing him were regularly punctuated by bursts of hearty and wholesome laughter; almost without exception at our own expense as we exchanged stories from our own experiences.

His dedication can be almost frightening at times, but it is always lightened by his humanity, which is never far away. For example, en route to Senegal for the Dakar Campaign in 1995, the Formula One Grand Prix championship had finally been settled by another fine performance from the German driver, Michael Schumacher. Reinhard's pleasure on hearing the news was plain for all to see, but it was equally clear on discussing it with him that it was only a passing interest. He can and does sometimes relax and he loves to play with his grandchildren. But his life's consuming passion is found in evangelism.

I am grateful to all members of the Christ for all Nations (CfaN) team, particularly Peter van den Berg, whose insights were enormously helpful; Rob and Vanessa Birkbeck for their technical assistance, research skills, compilation of the photo sections, and indeed for help in every part of the book's production.

In the final stages of the book the help of John Fergusson was invaluable and most timely. His inside knowledge of Reinhard's growing ministry in India was a revelation and his editorial skills much appreciated.

Last, but by no means least, my thanks to my dear wife Hazel, for her constant supply of practical wisdom and encouragement — and her patience in putting up with her reclusive husband throughout the writing of yet another book.

Nottingham, England, 1998

Colin Whittaker

Part One

Early Days

The Unfolding of a Dream

Reinhard was on the road to Lesotho again. Lesotho, where it had all begun. But no, there had been many other beginnings also! His mind was overflowing with a kaleidoscope of memories.

The highway from Johannesburg led straight to the mountain kingdom, five hours to the south. Huge grain silos swept by, incongruous giants in the sepia summer grass of the highveld. They passed scattered cement settlements hung about with washing. Men sat, waiting in the sunshine. He knew their lives and their hearts, and his own swelled with his deep love for this continent and its people.

The previous week, in March 1998, he had also been in Maseru, the capital of the tiny inland state of Lesotho. The beheaded hills, shrouded in luxuriant green bush, were achingly familiar. 'Moruti! Moruti Bonnke!' The welcome had been wonderful, unexpected. He had come to develop a new project, another means of reaching the world with the gospel. It had enormous potential, perhaps more than any other God had so far given him, and his whole being resonated with it: 'People must hear the gospel! People must get saved!'

He preached in the streets where he had ministered thirty years before. Then, a mere handful had come, but soul by precious soul, they had given their lives to Jesus. Today those men were themselves soul-winners and church-planters. What a privilege to serve the living God! For thirty years he had tramped the blood-red soils of Africa proclaiming the Good

News of Jesus Christ. And now a new generation, hungry for the gospel, pressed forward to catch a word of truth.

God was so faithful! Reinhard had begun here in Lesotho, with less than nothing. 'Below zero!' he described it, and God had enriched him with an uncountable harvest — millions upon millions of lives changed by the gospel of Jesus. Here too had come the unforgettable dream of a blood-washed Africa, and the words the Holy Spirit had whispered, 'Africa shall be saved!' that became his driving passion. God's promise, that he would preach from Cape Town to Cairo, had been greatly exceeded and yet remained to be fulfilled.

He remembered as yesterday his first visit to Cairo, in September 1995. What a month that had been! There had been the culmination of the Minus-to-Plus project in Germany; his first visit to Senegal; and then preaching not only in Jerusalem, but also Cairo.

Originally, that was to have been no more than an exploratory meeting with a few pastors after the World Pentecostal Conference in Jerusalem. But somehow news had leaked out and thousands had gathered from all parts of the Arabic-speaking nation.

When at last he had arrived at the church, he had been astonished. The building was crammed, and hundreds had to be turned away. What was happening in the busy, bustling capital of Muslim-dominated Egypt thrilled him beyond measure. Their response to the ministry had been humbling and heart-warming. Many responded. Many were healed. That preliminary meeting, wonderful though it had been, had merely sown the seed for a far mightier harvest. In God's time, he would be back to preach to millions, and the prospect stirred him to the depths of his being.

Five years earlier he had stood at the source of the Nile, where the broad, clear water surged from Lake Victoria in the heart of the continent. Standing on its banks he had prophesied that just as the Nile sweeps northwards to the sea, so shall the river of the Holy Spirit sweep into Cairo from the south. He remembered the occasion with a mixture of joy tinged with sadness, for that had been at Jinja, a campaign that had been prematurely halted by machine-gun toting militia. It had not been an easy journey, but every step had been a privilege.

Ahead of them the mountains of Lesotho soared into golden clouds, a parable of God's provision, and his destiny. Reinhard broke into spontaneous praise and thanksgiving: 'My God, my God, how fantastic, how absolutely fantastic.'

Jerusalem too had been excellent. For Reinhard, neither the symbolism nor the irony of the visit was lost. Jerusalem had been chosen as the 1995 venue for the World Pentecostal Conference, and Reinhard invited to be a keynote speaker. Although everyone knows he prefers gospel campaigns to conferences, he could not refuse that one. For Reinhard, as the son of a German army officer in the Second World War, to be able to speak in Jerusalem itself, the City of Zion, was too great a miracle of God to deny. He revelled in such situations, giving all the glory to God who makes them possible.

In that same month, Minus-to-Plus was climaxing in Germany. God had already placed in his heart even more daring plans for the future. 'Minus to Plus' for Scandinavia and Hong Kong in 1996; America and Canada in 1999! All the time the African campaigns would continue as God led. Other nations must not be neglected either. The world must be reached with the gospel. The latest thing to be stirring his heart and mind was to use the latest technology of Satellites and the internet to put out teaching on evangelism, to raise up a new generation of evangelists to take the message of salvation in Christ to the ends of the earth.

Was that already nearly three years ago? The memory of it bubbled up as fresh as a spring. It had been a remarkable call from God that had led him to launch the project to put a booklet into every home in the British Isles, and then in the whole of German-speaking Europe. Initially it had seemed ridiculous, and had not by any means proved easy. But the team had committed themselves to it, and had pressed on doggedly to see it through. Those were days of high financial drama.

'How much do we need today?' Reinhard remembered asking, the moment he returned to Frankfurt from Cairo. A figure was mentioned. There had been a silence around the room as the real nature of this life of faith sank in. He was always greatly encouraged by the faithfulness of those who had stood with him from the beginning — Werner and Lilo Bühler, Eugen Würslin, and so many others. He could read the faith on their faces, and it lifted his own. Then he had spread open his hands, stood to his feet and said, 'So. Let's pray.' The needs were colossal and they could only look to God. He remembered how faithfully he had provided. Not a single bill had been paid late, to the glory of God.

Nor was that all, of course. In a dozen cities scattered across the globe, committees were themselves industriously planning and praying in preparation for their coming event with evangelist Reinhard Bonnke. For them it would be the fruit of many months of labour and years of intercession, and one of the highlights of their lives. Then, too, there was the multitude of other literature projects, less well publicised, in which millions of books and booklets were being poured like rain into the spiritual deserts of the world into countries like China, the Sudan; Burma and Iran. All faced impossibilities, and all needed faithful prayer and, of course, money.

And the intervening years had not been idle either! Indeed, the pace continued to increase, and there were times when Reinhard's body screamed with tiredness. How long could he keep up the pace? But the fire in his spirit soon burned away all thoughts of rest.

Plans for the American booklet distribution had consumed his time, energy and resources in ways he had never before experienced. Often approaching the brink of giving up, each time God had faithfully seen them through.

They had continued to push back the frontiers of darkness in Africa, and his heart leaped at the new breakthrough in Nigeria. When he remembered his recent meeting with the president, who had offered him an open invitation to return to that needy and populous nation, he rejoiced. It was there in Kaduna that he had received God's promise that one day he would preach to a million souls in one meeting. Would that be in Lagos?

Or would it instead be in India? For that sub-continent was opening to the gospel like a flower in the sunshine. The recent campaigns in Colombo, Sri Lanka and Pune in India had been awesome. He had sensed a new spiritual climate and seen such a hunger for the truth that he believed India would now turn to Christ as had Africa. Sri Lanka had been in civil war for twelve years and a campaign there had seemed out of the question. And yet God had moved in the hearts of the local churches to expect a miracle, and it had come. Tens of thousands gave their lives to Jesus in what some said was the biggest gathering the island nation had ever seen.

The scene had been repeated in Pune, India, and most recently of all, in the capital, New Delhi. There were nearly a billion Indians, and for each one Christ had died. Already further campaigns were in preparation there, and his pulse quickened in anticipation.

Then, as ever, the urgency of the task almost overwhelmed him. He must press on towards the goal — to reach the lost of the world. There was so little time. For there could be no prize until every living being had heard the wonderful Good News of his Jesus. Jerusalem and Cairo, even America, were no finale. No, no, no! They were stepping-stones to the future.

As the car began winding into the foothills towards Maseru, once again he rejoiced, overflowing with praise. What a time to be alive! How wonderful to be serving God when the Holy Spirit was moving in such power in nation after nation.

But despite his expanding vision for the world, Africa would for ever hold a corner of his heart. From platforms across the continent he admitted, 'If you scratch my skin, underneath I am black!' Now as he anticipated another African campaign he thanked God that he was called to this.

A Way in the Desert

'No way,' John Darku had said. 'Senegal is completely closed.'

John was a gentle Ghanaian with a broad face and a bright smile. But he hadn't been smiling then. As the director responsible for preparing events throughout West Africa, John had discussed plans for the Dakar event with Reinhard Bonnke, and said, 'Even the pastors don't want a campaign.'

The year was 1994, and John had been patiently visiting the capital of Senegal for years. Reinhard had checked his *Operation World* on his laptop. Under 'Senegal', this former French colony which had gained independence in 1960, he read, 'Much of the land is arid with few natural resources ... Christians are few ... Islam has grown over the last 50 years ... Dakar has nearly two million out of a total population of some eight and a half million ... Roman Catholics 5.4% ... Evangelicals, Pentecostals and Charismatics only 0.11%.' It had not looked promising. But in faith an event had been pencilled in for September 1995.

Senegal was barren spiritually as well as naturally. Nevertheless, the dramatic cry, 'Africa shall be saved!' that had burst from the depths of Reinhard's being over twenty years before had found a fervent 'Amen' in the hearts of committed intercessors around the world — the CfaN prayer partners. Thousands had targeted Senegal in prayer and slowly attitudes there had begun to soften.

Planning a campaign in any part of Africa required wisdom, experience and not a little courage. The situation was constantly changing, and often lives could be in danger. Even the CfaN team had lost two precious members, but in faith Reinhard and John had initiated plans for the event and the dates were fixed.

Now nearly a year later, the news from Dakar was encouraging. A few pastors were now very keen. But the authorities stated that the proposed event could only be advertised as a music festival at which Reinhard would be allowed to speak. However the door was creaking open at last. Reinhard felt that the opportunity should be grabbed while there was a chance, and asked John to complete the work of planning and training the local churches. There was not much time left to build the necessary momentum.

When they finally touched down at Dakar airport, Reinhard and the team were given a very warm welcome by the Minister of the Interior, Christian pastors and a colourful crowd of two to three hundred local Christians, waving banners and singing as only Africans can. Reinhard was bundled into a waiting VIP Mercedes and, complete with police escort, sliced through the African melee to the hotel.

The following evening the team gathered for a welcome reception by the Evangelical Fellowship of Senegal. Government representatives rubbed shoulders with pastors and their wives in unprecedented unity. It was a grand occasion, and one could feel faith rising in the hearts of all present when Reinhard addressed the gathering. All was set. The event was under way. A way had been made in the desert.

Reinhard Bonnke leans forward on his seat on the platform, his Bible on his lap, his eyes fixed on the swelling crowd. He is praying under his breath as he waits to preach. Dust hangs in the air above the platform, the red, red dust of Africa. The crowds sway and clap to the weaving rhythms of the drums, rejoicing with the singers. Some of the drums are African but there is a

Western drum kit and a modern keyboard. The song leader breaks into joyful dancing as he sings. The excitement and expectancy in the air can be felt.

For German-born Reinhard Bonnke, this is home. Here, with the sweat trickling down his back and the smell of Africa in his nostrils; here, with his Bible in his hands, an eager, hungry crowd in front of him, and a platform from which to preach his beloved Jesus. This is what he lives for. This is what he would die for.

The moment arrives, and he jumps to his feet, takes the microphone, and cries, 'Hallelujah!' Right arm high, hand spread wide, he waves to the crowd, and cries again, 'Hallelujah! Hallelujah! Eh!'

Already the crowd responds with delight. Very soon Reinhard sheds any German reserve, and slips into his African mould. His interpreter follows every word, every gesture. Reinhard's deep love for the African people is quickly perceived, cutting through all barriers of language or culture. The Holy Spirit is at work through the missionary whose one burning motive is to introduce these precious people of Senegal to his Saviour.

By now the sun has disappeared behind the horizon with tropical suddenness. Rich hues of blood-red glory speak to all of the Creator's majesty. The attentive crowd relaxes in the warm night air. The first-night nerves of the pastors on the platform dissolve as they are gripped by the message. Above them, the moon soon sheds its silvery light over the crowd — a lesser light reflecting the brightness of the now invisible sun. On the platform another is faithfully reflecting the brightness of the unseen Son of God. Here is a true evangelist, a man of God who knows his calling is to reveal the one who is the Light of the world.

From first to last he preaches Jesus. The basic truths of the gospel come across with a loving simplicity. Fearlessly he preaches Christ as the only one who can save us from our sins through his death on the cross. The Bible is the word of God. Jesus is the Son of God. His miraculous birth, his sinless life, his sacrificial death, his resurrection and ascension, are declared with absolute conviction and without apology.

Most of the crowd has been standing for over three hours, but when the appeal to receive Christ as Saviour is made there is a special stillness. The Holy Spirit is moving. New lives are being born in the sultry African night. This is the supreme moment — a holy moment. It is as though all heaven is waiting with bated breath, waiting to join in the 'Amen'. His shirt soaked with perspiration, Reinhard leads them carefully through a prayer of commitment. He concludes with these words, 'Jesus is the Son of God. I believe it. I receive it, and I thank you for it. Amen.' The crowd, many in tears, repeat the words step by step after the interpreters. It is done, but it is not finished.

All who have responded are next given one of the follow-up booklets by the counsellors. Priority is always given to salvation. No one is ever left in any doubt that this is of paramount importance. But signs and wonders are an essential confirmation of the preached word if a real impact is to be made in a Muslim-dominated country such as Senegal. Reinhard prays for the sick in his campaigns because he believes it is part of the gospel of Christ.

He returns to the microphone. 'Bonnke is not the healer. Jesus is the healer,' he explains. He urges the crowd to look to Christ for their healing as he prays a general prayer for all the sick who are present. Then under the anointing of the Holy Spirit he begins to mention specific afflictions such as deafness, dumbness, blindness, arthritis, crippled limbs, and 'in the name of Jesus' he encourages them to receive their healing. All the time he is praying there is a deep stillness over the whole crowd. He urges them to test what God has done, and to share it with their friends. Soon excited little groups gather where people have been healed.

'Come to the platform and tell us what Jesus has done for you,' Bonnke urges. The outstanding cases are verified and testify convincingly of healing from blindness and deafness, and several who have been deaf and dumb can hear and speak a few words. It is a promising start to a pioneer campaign.

Reinhard retires to the waiting car exhausted, but his spirit is singing. When he returns to his hotel, he will shower and change, but sleep will probably elude him as it so often does when the Holy Spirit is burning within him. He will write, and pray, and study the word of God until drowsiness finds him at last.

After an early breakfast the following morning, the team met for devotions in Reinhard's room, as is their custom in these campaigns. As always, Bonnke expounded a chapter of Scripture. It was all so delightfully informal, so different from his platform preaching, but it was powerful, searching and faith-building, revealing his delight in the word of God. When Reinhard opens his Bible and shares from his heart, it is fresh and inspiring. Familiar scriptures burst into new life. Afterwards, there was earnest prayer for a mighty move of God in Senegal. It surely would come.

In answer to their prayers, the crowds increased, the miracles bringing wonder and rejoicing to their hearts. And throughout the week thousands responded to the call for salvation. By the weekend, the whole city was alive with the talk of the town — this Jesus and the miracles that are done in his name. The nation that had been totally closed, where before there had been no way, had received the touch of the finger of God. As the technicians dismantled the equipment, the rain storm which had held off all week swept the city, as though in confirmation that this event had been planned in heaven.

On the final morning the team broke bread together, thanking God for an excellent pioneer campaign. Reinhard confided, 'My spirit is soaring. I feel we have started something. They want us to return and I want to return.'

The Dakar event had by no means been outstanding compared with earlier campaigns. Nor perhaps was it a major turning point in the life of Reinhard Bonnke. But there is never anything ordinary about God's work, and for many thousands that week it was the moment they were rescued from the path to hell, the supreme event of their lives. They will never be the same. This is the powerful privilege of the evangelist.

There is a picture which lingers in the mind; a picture of Reinhard Bonnke straining forwards in his chair on the platform, his eyes sweeping the crowd of African faces in front of him, patiently waiting for the moment to preach his Saviour. His hands are folded together around the worn Bible in his lap. Total fulfilment is reflected in the earnestness and joy written in the lines of his face. At such times, does he ever wish that his father ... his soldier father ... could have been there beside him? How he would have loved these campaigns. Reinhard owed him so much. Both his father and his beloved mother had played such a vital part in preparing him for the service of God in evangelism.

Chapter 3

Refugees

Hermann Bonnke was born on 7th February 1905, in the city of Königsberg, on the Pregel river. Today it is Kaliningrad, near the cold Baltic coast of western Russia. But before the First World War, it was the capital of Prussia.

The Bonnke family were good Lutherans, and proud of it. The influence of Martin Luther and the Reformation was still felt after four centuries. But the authority of the Bible had been severely challenged by the so-called Higher Criticism of German theologians which was rife in the pre-war period. For many, it was faith-destroying. Instead, it was felt that intellectualism would educate the ignorance out of mankind and lead the world into peace and the millennium.

By the end of the war in 1918, Hermann was thoroughly disillusioned. Like most German youth of the day he found defeat a bitter pill to swallow. All the sacrifices they had been called to make for the war effort had been in vain. Church attendance suffered. If the Bible was full of myths, as the clever critics declared, what was there to hold on to? Was there even a God? Perhaps the atheistic Communists, now in power in Russia, were right.

Instead of getting better, things continued to get worse. The Bonnke family now found themselves facing new enemies of disease and debt. Weakened by years of inadequate food supply many of their friends fell easy prey to the worldwide flu epidemic which swept away more victims than the war itself. Then in 1923, when Germany could not pay the huge reparations imposed following the Treaty of Versailles, France occupied the Ruhr, and the German currency collapsed.

Understandably, Hermann had developed into a bitter and tough teenager. Whatever his family said, now that he was seventeen, he was determined to join the army as a volunteer. His parents still attended the local church, but that had long since lost its appeal to him. He had other ideas for his life.

So in 1923 he became a soldier in the Wermacht. But his joy was short-lived. One day to his horror, he began coughing up blood. He was shattered. Not only was TB incurable, but he dared not tell anyone for it would mean the end of his military career when it had barely begun.

Meanwhile, although his hopes were being destroyed, something had happened to his family, giving them fresh hope. They had been invited to a local event to hear an American Pentecostal evangelist. Herr Bonnke and his wife, Hermann's parents, had instant misgivings. However, Hermann's father suffered a great deal from rheumatism, and it was said that this American preacher prayed for the sick, and that people were getting healed. Finally they were persuaded, and not only was Herr Bonnke healed, but both he and his wife received Christ as their Saviour and Lord.

At the first opportunity they told Hermann the wonderful news. He was not interested. But his disease was getting worse, and he wouldn't be able to conceal it much longer. Finally he too agreed to attend, telling God that if he healed him he would give his life to follow this Jesus. When the evangelist laid hands on him he was healed, and yielded his life to Christ. The whole family rejoiced.

The 1920s were troubled years for Europe. The idealism of the immediate post-war period was fading rapidly. Soaring inflation and unemployment were sowing seeds of discontent, and Hitler began his rise to power. Within two years of his conversion, Hermann Bonnke wanted to leave the army and spend his whole life serving the Lord, but to his dismay he found he was locked firmly into the army for life. That being so, he determined to be the best he could as an officer and Christian, and soon became known as the Preaching Officer. Like most of his countrymen, he was unaware of the looming crisis.

In 1933, he met and married the young organist at their church, Meta Scheffler. Seven years his junior, she was just twenty-one, and a talented singer and tailoress. Their first child, Martin, was born the next year, followed by Gerhard two years later. Life was good. They had a secure salary and home, and their faith was growing. Hermann was not ashamed of his Pentecostal convictions. In spite of the Berlin Declaration of 1909 by the Evangelicals denouncing Pentecostalism, he searched the Scriptures for himself and came to his own conclusions about the reality of the baptism of the Holy Spirit and the gifts of the Spirit, including the controversial gift of tongues.

At this time, Hermann found few conflicts between his army and Christian life. His duties were in the area of supplies and logistics — from food to fuel and uniforms to blankets. However, as Hitler's intentions became clearer during the late 1930s, he was increasingly concerned. But Hitler's propaganda machine was effective, and deceived many, including the churches who continued to pray for him and his government. A few brave souls spoke out, but were silenced or simply disappeared. There were rumours of 'special camps', but few believed them. Then suddenly, Germany found itself at war once more.

Hermann was kept extremely busy during those momentous days of early 1940. The German armies were advancing on every front, stretching the supply lines to their limit. When he had a moment, he registered the birth of their fifth son, Reinhard Willi Gottfried Bonnke, born on 19th April. Martin was already nearly seven and his father was very proud of him. His hopes

were resting on his oldest son to become a great preacher. The
year before, Meta had been delivered of twins, Jürgen and Peter.
This newest child? Well, there would be plenty of time to see
what he would do.

In their fine army home, Meta was delighted with her latest
son. She was a wonderful mother and proudly displayed son
number five to his older brothers. She used to sing and play the
piano, and she loved to sew. She had secretly longed for a
daughter for whom she could make pretty frocks, but she was
content with her family.

By now, Hermann had divided loyalties. Part of him was
proud of the military successes, but as a Christian he was more
and more troubled by the news. As he listened to Goebbels
(Hitler's minister of propaganda) on the radio he wondered even
more. When Hitler broke his non-aggression pact with Russia,
the opening of the Eastern Front seriously alarmed Reinhard's
father. Not only was it a huge logistical challenge, but defeat
there could prove disastrous. Soon Hermann's unit was hard
pressed. Greatcoats, blankets, winter boots, fuel and anti-freeze
were as vital as weapons and ammunition, and were not easy to
obtain.

Throughout 1942 and 1943 personal supplies were equally
hard to come by, and things became increasingly difficult for
Meta and her family. Staple items, like soap, became luxuries.
The war began to turn against Germany, and Goebbels was no
longer convincing. Secretly, and not a little afraid, Hermann
began to listen to the BBC radio. What he heard confirmed his
worst fears. Germany was losing the war. He also learned what
he had begun to suspect — that Jews were being systematically
exterminated. It was too awful to contemplate. He plucked up
his courage and confronted a senior officer, who rounded on him
and told him, 'Shut your mouth immediately. Keep quiet or you
will find yourself along with the Jews and be killed with them.'
He was deeply shaken.

In July, 1942, Meta bore the girl she had wanted for so long. But the war was beginning to turn against Germany and two years after the birth of their duaghter, Felicitas, by the summer of 1944, defeat was inevitable. News came which sent a chill of fear through the whole family. The Russians had reached the borders of Germany. Now a Major, Hermann feared for his young family. What would happen to them?

Meta was a woman of prayer, confident that God would take care of them. But Hermann had heard of the terrible revenge the Russians were exacting on their foes as they advanced. They could not expect mercy if they fell into their hands.

'Meta, be ready to evacuate at short notice,' he warned his wife as he left for duty one evening. She began to make rucksacks for each of her boys. She talked and prayed with them, but still couldn't accept that she may have to leave her lovely home. As night fell, little Reinhard looked out of his bedroom window and shouted excitedly to his mother to come and see the bonfires that were burning in the distance, lighting up the sky. He wanted his Papa to see them too, but the Major was away on duty. The retreating German army was in chaos. Reinhard would not see his father again for four years.

Suddenly there was a loud knock on the door and Meta jumped. She composed herself and opened to a surprised German soldier. He was in a state of panic, and shocked to see her.

'Woman, what are you doing here? Don't you know the danger? The Russians are coming!' By then Reinhard and his brothers had gathered behind her.

'You must leave now, before it is too late. There is just one way still open out of the city, but for how long who knows? If you are still here when the Russians come.' His face said it all.

'Thank you for warning us,' she said, and closed the door. What should she do? As always she prayed, and as she did she knew they must leave, and at once. To the boys, packing was an adventure. Meta ran to a neighbour. All her complacency had left her. The ring of fire round the city was getting nearer, the gunfire louder, and she could see others hurriedly leaving. Her neighbour and her five children were all ready to leave, and didn't need a second telling.

The two women and their brood of eleven children made their way to the main road. Carrying her baby daughter, Meta shepherded the boys, urging them to keep close together. It was chaos on the escape road with miles of army lorries. They were nose-to-tail and packed to capacity with battle-weary, defeated soldiers intent on trying to save their own skins. Along the sides of the road trudged hundreds of escaping civilians, loaded with whatever possessions they could carry. Meta and her friend waved frantically to every passing lorry, pleading with the drivers to stop, but in vain. She was beginning to despair when at last one slowed. It was full of soldiers. The two women had agreed that they would not be separated, and before the soldiers could argue they were loading their children onto the lorry. Little Reinhard soon found himself sitting on the lap of a big German soldier.

'Halt, halt ... no more ... we are overloaded now.' But the two determined mothers overcame all protests and succeeded against all the odds in desperately pushing every one of their children on board, before scrambling on themselves.

The progress on the road was slow and dangerous. They were making for Danzig (now Gdansk), 160 km to the west. Meta's parents lived there, and she felt if they could get to the coast they would have a better chance to escape. Just when they were beginning to feel safe, they heard the sound of aeroplanes. They could feel the soldiers around them stiffen with fear, and with good reason, for they recognised the sound of Russian planes. Suddenly the night sky was lit up around them. The covering cloak of darkness was whisked away as the planes dropped their flares. The note of the planes' engines changed as they prepared to dive-bomb and strafe the retreating army. Throughout the night the sky was lit up with dazzling lights, the sounds of crumpled explosions, the rattle of conflict. Tracer bullets arched through the clouded sky as if probing and searching for a target in the darkness. Young as he was, it was an experience Reinhard will never forget.

Eventually as daylight dawned the two families found a spot in a wooded area where they could rest, and they dispatched their older children to look for firewood so they could cook some porridge. Reinhard decided he would help as well, so off he trotted. He found a few sticks and proudly moved on collecting more. But when he looked around he could no longer see his mother or brothers. He panicked. He was lost. He started to scream and run, but he was running further and further away from his mother. There were refugees everywhere in the forest, but none he recognised.

At last a kind woman saw him and gathered him in her arms. Between sobs he told her he was lost and he wanted his mother. By now she was searching too, and from the vantage point of the woman's arms, he saw her in the distance. In a trice he wriggled free and ran back to the welcome of his frightened mother.

The hand of God was upon them, and eventually they arrived exhausted at a place on the coast of the Haff Sea. Here the sea often freezes in winter, and there is a narrow channel used as a crossing place for horse-drawn carts, cars and lorries. When the refugees arrived it was nearing the end of winter, and the ice was thawing. But in the desperation, vehicles of all kinds were still crossing over to Danzig. The melting ice had made it dangerous with slush, but encircled by the Russians, thousands were taking the risk. It was the only escape route still open.

To their huge relief, the families managed to get a ride on a military truck which was fleeing across the ice. Once again the children were bundled in, and the two women prayed as the truck slithered precariously over the melting sea. The ice creaked and cracked. Cold and frightened but very relieved, they made it to Danzig at last where they met with Meta's sister and mother. Reinhard's grandmother was a devout Christian and it was a joyful if tearful reunion. They had no idea where Major Bonnke was. They hoped fervently that he had not been captured by the Russians, and thanked God for bringing them safely across the frozen sea. Later they heard the awful news that the Russians had bombed the crossing place breaking up the ice and plunging thousands of refugees and soldiers to their death in the icy waters.

Danzig was packed with refugees trying to find a ship to take them westwards away from the approaching conflict. A ship called the Gustlov was in the harbour, but it was already overloaded with several thousand on board. It steamed slowly out into the Baltic to Denmark. It never made it. Two days later the news reached Danzig that it had been sunk by a torpedo from a Russian submarine.

The situation in the city deteriorated rapidly. Russian planes were bombing the city. Then the families found a place on an old coal steamer. They needed no urging to pray. In such circumstances, flowery phrases and long-winded petitions are discarded. The Bible suddenly becomes a handbook of hope in hopeless situations.

The two women prayed and one took a promise from a Bible promise box. They opened the slip of paper and read out, 'Thus saith the Lord which maketh a way in the sea, and a path in the mighty waters' (Isaiah 43:16, AV). It was as though God had spoken audibly to their trembling hearts. They knelt and committed themselves and their children into the hands of God. It was a promise they had to cling to.

The little group made their way to the harbour and found the gangplank a seething mass of humanity, desperate to get aboard.

Somehow they made it through the pushing, shoving and shouting, and found their berth below deck, as the air raid sirens warned of another attack.

Reinhard was just under five years old, but the journey was unforgettable. They were packed in with hundreds of other passengers. Conditions were not good and as the ship steamed slowly out to sea, many became sick and everyone was afraid. They soon heard the sound of Russian aeroplanes. Several times they were attacked, but survived.

The toilet was on deck, and Reinhard had to go. He struggled up the vomit-covered vertical ladder. On deck, peering through the rails, he watched as a Russian plane was shot down and fell in flames into the sea. Two days later the ship shuddered with a huge explosion. It had struck a mine and began to list badly. The women prayed, the promise from Isaiah firm in their hearts. Then to their relief the ship miraculously righted itself and limped on into the Danish port.

They were overwhelmed when they finally stepped ashore, safe on Danish soil, and they praised God for their great deliverance. At first they were treated well, but within weeks Germany surrendered, and the family were interned in a refugee camp. They were to be there for three and a half years. The war was over, but many of their struggles were just beginning.

Meanwhile, Hermann was relieved to discover that Meta and the children had escaped from Königsberg. He hoped against hope that they had been able to reach safety. It was to be a long time before he would know.

Hitler had insisted that Königsberg be a fortress city to stem the Russian advance, and Hermann had no choice but to stay. By the end of January 1945, the German troops were trapped with their backs to the Baltic Sea. On the 30th March, news filtered through that Danzig, where Hermann had hoped his family might be, had fallen to the Russians. He feared deeply for their safety. Within a few days the Russian assault on Königsberg began, and raged for three terrible days. The outcome was inevitable. The memories of those awful days never left Hermann Bonnke. He resolved that if he and his family ever survived, he would instil in them the horrors of war.

When it became clear that the city was doomed, he was allowed to evacuate, being the father of six children. Gathering important papers, he boarded one of the last ships to leave, a German minesweeper. While still at sea, they heard of the German capitulation, and Hermann ditched his papers in the sea. They were taken by a British warship to Kiel, North Germany, where they were interned in a prisoner of war camp. He was there for nine months, and while conditions were harsh with very little food, they were better than those of many colleagues who had been sent to Siberia by the Russians, but he longed to know if his family were alive.

As a German and committed Christian Hermann Bonnke was deeply ashamed and broken in spirit when news came of the horror of the extermination camps. He pondered long and hard how such a great nation, of which he had always been so proud to be a part, could have allowed such evil to take over its soul. He had always been a man of prayer with a great love for the Bible, and these revelations served to drive him closer to God and deepen his faith.

He resolved that given the opportunity he would spend the remainder of his days preaching the gospel. One night in the camp, as he was lying on his bed with his eyes open, the door opened and the Lord Jesus Christ appeared to him. He was not asleep. The Lord Jesus walked over to him and said, 'I am so glad you are coming.' To Hermann it was clear confirmation of his desire to become a preacher of the gospel and he wept and wept.

Through the Red Cross he eventually heard to his great joy that Meta and the children had made it safely to a refugee camp in Denmark. He hurriedly wrote, but it would be years before they were reunited.

Meta's faith and courage did not fail her during those testing years. It was not easy. Many Danes felt strongly about the Germans in the camp and some actually attacked the camp with revenge in mind. Fortunately they were guarded safely and kept from harm by the Danish military. The inmates tried to make the best of a bad situation. They soon learned that they had lost their homes for ever. Germany had been divided by the Allied Forces, and large parts of eastern Germany had gone to Poland.

Martin, the eldest in the Bonnke family, now eleven years old, asked his mother the inevitable question: 'Mama when are we going home to Königsberg?'

She hated to have to tell him, 'Martin, no one knows when we shall leave this camp, but now I must tell you that we will never be going back to our lovely home in Königsberg. East Prussia where the Bonnke families have lived for so long is now part of Russia. They have even changed the name to Kaliningrad. We must be brave and remember that God will continue to take care of us in these hard times. And Martin, because you are the eldest, and with Papa away, you must help me to look after your brothers and sister.'

The camp managed to arrange some very basic schooling for the children, though the teachers were unqualified. Food was rationed, and accommodation was basic, with two or three families sharing a chalet. Each day the children helped carry water from some distance away. Money was non-existent and everyone used vouchers. There were no luxuries.

But despite these hardships, the Bonnke family were extremely fortunate, for Meta thrived on adversity. She soon organised a choir, copying out the music by hand, and used her faith to lift the spirits of all around her. Whenever she discovered that it was someone's birthday, she would take her choir to sing 'Happy Birthday' outside their chalet. One year, on her own birthday, Meta was able to visit a Lutheran church in the area. She was thrilled when she saw the large pipe organ.

'Sir,' she asked the minister, 'would you consider giving me a present?' He was taken aback, saying he had nothing, but she continued, 'Please would you allow me to play one piece on the organ? That would be a wonderful birthday present for me.' He agreed, no doubt relieved at getting off so lightly. But when he heard her play, it was his turn to ask Meta for a favour. 'Please would you come and play the organ in our services?' She was delighted to accept.

Her sewing skills were also much in demand, every garment being patched and passed down. Reinhard was the fifth boy. Meta watched her children growing up. How many more birthdays must they spend in this internment camp in Denmark? Martin was now a teenager. She continued to pray that God would open the way for them to return to Germany, although conditions on the outside were still terrible. The letters from Hermann helped, but they were long, tiresome, trying days. The extended separation was painful for all of them.

At last they were transferred to Poppendorf, a camp in northern Germany, and it was here at long last that Reinhard was reunited with his father. The young boy was almost nine, and although he hadn't seen his Papa for nearly four years he recognised him immediately in the distance. What a joyful reunion. Their release soon followed, and the children were so excited to be saying goodbye to the camp.

Hermann had found a single room for all of them, in the small town of Glückstadt, in northern Germany, not far from Hamburg, and he was lucky to find that. Along with most of the inhabitants of that small town by the River Elbe, they experienced real poverty. The quarters were so cramped that eventually some of the children had to sleep elsewhere. But they thanked God that they were together with their father. He filled the long evenings with stories of the horrors of war, and to this day, when the subject comes up, Reinhard Bonnke says with a strength of expression fermented from those years, 'War is hell. It is awful.' Although a true German, he adds with deep conviction, 'I am glad the Allies defeated Hitler. If they had not done so, he would have destroyed every Jew.' Those years created in Reinhard an empathy for refugees, the poor and persecuted that would live in his heart for ever. He learned another vital lesson also.

Chapter 4

The Spirit-filled Boy

Although their one room accommodation in Glückstadt was cramped, life gradually began to assume some form of normality for the first time since the end of the war. As soon as possible Hermann and Meta got their six children enrolled in school. Martin, now fifteen years of age, led the way, followed by Gerhard (thirteen), and the twins Jürgen and Peter (ten), then Reinhard (nine) and their little sister Felicitas (seven).

It was quite an ordeal for all of them, for it was soon evident that they were behind the other children after the scrappy schooling they had received in the camp. However, they were bright and though it was a struggle for the first few months, ultimately all of them excelled in their studies.

Slowly things began to improve. There was so much that was different from life in the camp. Money for example. In the camp they had to rely on hand-outs for everything. They had no money. It was a new experience for Reinhard to go shopping with Meta and watch her buy things. Even though the shops were poorly stocked, it seemed wonderful after the camps. He quickly realised the value of money. One very special delight was the sweets. Even Martin could hardly remember sweets and chocolate. Little Reinhard found them irresistible — and his mother's purse too easily accessible for his suddenly sticky fingers. He got away with it once or twice but then his mother found him out. Reinhard was sure he was in for a smacking.

Meta had looked after the children by herself for the last four years, and it had not been straightforward. She did not hesitate to hand out a smart slap if the occasion arose. To 'spare the rod was to spoil the child'. Meta loved all of them dearly but typically for German parents of the period, she did not find it easy to demonstrate her love in frequent displays of hugs and kisses. However, just once a year, on their birthdays, each child knew he could count on a wonderful, long hug from their mother. Reinhard looked forward to that as much as, if not more than, any of his other birthday presents. He says, 'To be hugged by her on my birthday was like heaven.'

At this particular moment, however, he was both ashamed and afraid. He waited for the smack he knew he deserved. But Meta was not only a caring mother, albeit a fairly strict one, she was also a deeply committed Christian who longed for her children to know the Lord as their own Saviour as she did. She realised she must handle this situation sensitively as well as firmly. Reinhard was growing up. She did not make the common mistake of under-estimating the spiritual capacity of a boy of nine.

Breathing a prayer, she sat her 'delinquent' young son down and started to talk to him. At first Reinhard was relieved. But as Meta looked straight into his eyes, he was not so sure that this was not worse than the anticipated smacking.

'Reinhard, you know it is wrong to steal. Doing this means you are on your way to hell.' Reinhard gulped and listened hard. 'This is why Jesus came into the world, to save sinners. This is why he had to die on the cross, to save us from our sins.'

For the first time in his young life Reinhard understood that he was a sinner and that he needed Jesus to save him. To this day Reinhard remembers every detail. He says, 'At that moment something happened in my heart. That was the moment of my salvation when she prayed for me. That was the last time I stole.'

Meta went on to remind Reinhard that he must now confess Christ as his Saviour in the church service on Sunday. That is what their church expected of everyone who claimed to have accepted Christ privately. For Reinhard, that did not present a problem. On Sunday when the pastor made the appeal he responded openly, sealing what Christ had already done in his heart.

Hermann and Meta rejoiced, the evidence of a work of grace in Reinhard was plain to see. Things were changing for the better for all of them in very many ways. To their huge relief, they were able to get better accommodation. They had experienced real poverty, but Reinhard never regrets those years. They served to create within him a kindred feeling for the millions of the world's poor which has never left him. Neither has the necessity for absolute honesty where money is concerned. The incident with his mother's purse was the start of a lifetime of total integrity in all money matters. The Master Potter was patiently shaping a vessel for his honour.

For Hermann, too, life suddenly improved. Even after the war it had seemed that there was no escape from a lifetime of soldiering. But his heart was in praying and preaching — in that order. He longed to be free to serve God as a pastor, and God saw his heart. Konrad Adenauer, then Chancellor of West Germany, was able to ensure that long-serving regulars would receive a pension for life if they chose to leave the army. Hermann did not have to think twice! He left with an army pension at the age of forty-four.

He applied to become a pastor with a section of the Pentecostal Church in Germany, and pioneered a church in Krempe, a small community of some two thousand inhabitants about five miles from their home in Glückstadt. Krempe was regarded as an outstation of the Hamburg Pentecostal Church.

Hermann was in his element. In common with many families in 1950, they did not possess a car, but Hermann had a bicycle and he enjoyed the exercise of cycling the five miles each way. However, Meta and the children had to attend the Glückstadt church.

Despite his nickname 'The Preaching Major', Hermann was not a particularly good preacher. He often stuttered and stammered as he started preaching, but he had a burning heart and gave himself to prayer and fasting, and God spoke through him. God blessed his efforts in Krempe and the pioneer church started to grow into a small revival. Many were saved and healed. But his family suffered once again, his older sons especially resenting his long absences. It seemed that the 'church' had robbed them of their father.

It was a sad day for Hermann when he realised that his older sons were not showing a keen interest in Christianity. He had especially set his hopes on Martin, the eldest, becoming a great preacher. Martin was the most gifted, the brightest, the smartest; in fact he seemed to have the most of everything. Strangely it seems that, like Jesse with his son David, Reinhard did not figure in his plans at this stage; he was still too young, a mere child.

By the time Reinhard had received his next annual big hug from Meta on his tenth birthday, he was already showing a great interest in missionaries and the mission fields of the world. He loved reading about these servants of God who had left everything to go across the seas to preach the gospel to those who had never heard of Jesus.

So Reinhard was excited when it was announced in the church in Glückstadt that next week some missionaries would be speaking at the services. (Hermann, of course, would miss hearing them because, as always, he would be faithfully preaching out at Krempe.) Reinhard could hardly wait for Sunday to come.

He was captivated as they preached and shared their missionary experiences. As he listened, he heard another voice in his own heart telling him very clearly that one day he would preach the gospel in Africa. Today, Reinhard cannot remember who the missionaries were, or which mission field they were from, but he cannot forget that moment in the middle of the service when God spoke to him in his heart about Africa. It remains vividly with him as though recorded deep in his memory by a laser beam.

Reinhard was sure that it was the voice of God. It was such a powerful experience that he could not wait to tell his father. As soon as Hermann returned from the day's services in Krempe, Reinhard ran to him shouting, 'Papa, Papa, God spoke to me and told me that one day I must preach the gospel in Africa.' Hermann's response was somewhat deflating: 'Son, how do you know that God has called you?' he asked him. And for a whole year Hermann continued to question Reinhard about his 'call'.

Eventually Reinhard plucked up enough courage to ask him, 'Papa, how does it feel when someone has a real call from God since you don't seem to think that I have one?' His father replied, 'Son, when you have a real call from God then you know it, you know it deep in your heart. You know it and it cannot be shaken.'

Reinhard looked up at his father and said, 'Papa, I know I have a real call from God. I know, I know, I know.' Hermann was nonplussed by such a confident assertion coming from one so young. But later when Reinhard was in Africa, Hermann loved to relate that story with shining eyes and a proud father's heart.

In those post-war years there was a very real tendency among some German Pentecostal leaders to 'keep their foot on the brake'. Because of the 1909 Berlin Declaration, they were still treated with suspicion by most Evangelicals. Later on, Hitler had made things very difficult for Pentecostals by forcing them to amalgamate with the Baptists, so that manifestations of the gifts of the Spirit, especially speaking in other tongues, were not overly encouraged in the services. The inclination was towards order and respectability. And although the experience of the baptism of the Holy Spirit was fundamental to Pentecostalism, special services 'for seekers' were somewhat rare.

Fortunately for Reinhard his father was a convinced Pentecostal. To this day Reinhard honours the memory of his father, especially his stand for truth in the face of bitter and sustained opposition. Hermann Bonnke stood firm because after years of studying the Scriptures he could see no alternative. As a Pentecostal pastor in post-war Germany he remained steadfast when others found the price too high.

Reinhard's father had been baptised with the Holy Spirit when he was still in Königsberg. But his mother, Meta, had never received this experience. Over the years she had prayed and been prayed for without success, but she did not give up. In 1951 a special meeting was announced for those seeking to be filled with the Holy Spirit. It was not easy for Meta to go. Everyone in a Pentecostal church took it for granted that the pastor's wife was surely filled with the Holy Spirit! She listened once again to the explanatory talk from the Scriptures on how to receive the gift of the Holy Spirit. But no, there was nothing new. The 'gifted' person prayed for her, but to no avail. Once again she left disappointed.

Meta returned home and went to bed, but she could not sleep. Then suddenly the Lord Jesus, the Baptiser with the Holy Spirit, met with her. She 'went off like a rocket', praising God in other languages. She continued long and loud speaking in other tongues. The older boys in their own bedrooms heard their mother having this wonderful time speaking in tongues, but Reinhard slept on, oblivious.

Next morning Meta had to leave early for Hamburg, but she had time to put a note on the breakfast table, 'Dear Children, last night Jesus baptised me with the Holy Spirit. Mother.'

Reinhard could not wait for his mother to return home that evening from Hamburg. He ran to meet her and she hugged him — and it wasn't his birthday. Something must have happened!

'Mama,' he asked, 'did you have the flame of fire on your head?'

She chuckled at his question. 'No Reinhard, I didn't have the flame of fire, but I did speak in other tongues, and it is wonderful.'

The whole family rejoiced with her because they all knew how long she had been seeking. Hermann was delighted, for he knew that it would help her status in the church as a pastor's wife. Reinhard was happy for her too, but he could not hide his disappointment that she did not have the flame of fire on her head.

By now his older brothers were finding the persecution due to their Pentecostal background more than they could bear and were showing signs of dropping away from church. Hermann must have wondered whether any of his children would stand the test. But Reinhard was the very opposite of his brothers, and Hermann was at last beginning to recognise that God's hand was resting upon young Reinhard.

Later that year (1951) it was announced that an outstanding Finnish Pentecostal preacher, Revd Kukula, was coming to Glückstadt, and he had a special ministry of leading people into the baptism of the Holy Spirit. Hermann therefore decided to ask Reinhard whether he would like to accompany him to this special service.

Reinhard needed no second invitation — he desperately wanted this blessing. The memory of the way his mother, Meta, had been wonderfully filled with the Holy Spirit after her many years of seeking, was still fresh in his memory. He had seen the difference it had made in his mother's life and he was thirsting for the same experience. Young as he was, he knew that if he was going to be a missionary in Africa he needed the power of the Holy Spirit in his life. Reinhard was thrilled that his father had invited him to go with him. He was very excited.

When they arrived at the place where the service was to be held, Reinhard felt as though he was stepping into the New Jerusalem. Pastor Kukula stood to speak, and Reinhard hung on his every word. Kukula gave only a short message and then he asked the people who were seeking to be filled with God's Spirit to kneel and pray.

No sooner had Reinhard got on his knees than the power of God came upon him. He did not need anyone to lay hands upon him and no one did. The Christ, described by John the Baptist as the one 'who will baptise with the Holy Spirit', met with him. The Spirit surged within him and he burst forth in other tongues inspired by the joy in his eager young heart. It was like a heavenly fountain opening within him, the beginning of a flow which has never ceased.

From the time that the promise of the Spirit was fulfilled in him it became an on-going constant filling. In his own words: 'The whole experience boosted my faith like super-charging a car engine. The Bible tallied with what was happening. It was such a marvellous thing to me that I've never doubted since that miracles are for today.'

Whenever he is asked, 'When did you begin to see miracles in your ministry and why do so many turn to Christ when you preach?' his answer is always the same: 'God gives us the power to do what he commands. That comes through the baptism with the Holy Spirit.'

Reinhard's desire for God increased. He already realised that prayer was a key to releasing the power of God. Now he longed to attend the Friday prayer meeting at Glückstadt, but children were considered too young to understand the mysteries of

prayer. Prayer was for grown-ups. He tried everything he knew
to persuade his mother to let him go with her. As each Friday
drew near, Reinhard tried hard to be good. All the children took
a share in the household duties, such as washing up and even
darning socks. But now he volunteered to do extra dish washing,
and extra sock darning. As the time approached, Reinhard asked
if he could please go. He was so disappointed when she refused.

Meta did not treat his request too seriously at first. But one
Friday when she again refused he could not control his tears of
disappointment. She looked at him in astonishment. 'This is
amazing,' she said. 'My son is crying because he is not allowed
to attend the prayer meeting.' She looked at his tear-streaked
face and promised him, 'Reinhard from this day you may attend
all the prayer meetings and all the services you wish.' And he
did, with great joy. From that day forward he walked with his
mother to the prayer meetings, and in his own words, 'it was
absolutely wonderful'. He quickly became involved in all the
church activities. His brothers increasingly went their own
ways, but for Reinhard the church became his life. He loved
every part of it and entered into it whole-heartedly.

Meta was a gifted musician and Reinhard had inherited
something of her talent. She recruited him for the guitar choir,
and for the four part choir. He loved praising God in song. He
discovered that he had a natural ear for music, and could play
most tunes by ear. Music and evangelism are well-nigh
inseparable and the development of this natural talent under his
mother's skilled musicianship was invaluable.

From the time that he was about fourteen years old, Reinhard
started to accompany his father every Sunday to the services at
Krempe, travelling with him on the train, and the bond between
father and son deepened. They would leave in the morning, not
returning home until late at night after a full day together.
Services occupied much of the day but in between they would
spend time with families in the church for meals.

During one prayer meeting led by his father, Reinhard suddenly felt as though his fingers had been pushed into an electric power socket. It seemed to him as though his hands were full of electricity and he wondered what was happening to him. While he was still trying to puzzle it all out, he heard the Holy Spirit telling him to go and lay his hands upon a certain woman who was sitting on the opposite side of the prayer meeting. Reinhard did not want to do it. His father was strict; he was still a mixture between a German officer and an old-style Pentecostal pastor — a formidable combination indeed! Although everyone was encouraged to pray, there was no room for anyone but the pastor to minister and lead. Up to this time Reinhard had done no ministering because 'the pastor does it all' was the accepted order of things. The very thought of crossing over to pray for the woman on the opposite side of the prayer meeting left him petrified.

He stayed where he was. He could not do it. What would his father say if he suddenly got up and went to pray for this woman? What would his father do? What would the other people think and say? What would this woman say? He did not even know whether she was sick and in need of prayer. He was shy and he was still only a boy. No, he could not do it.

But as he stayed on his knees it seemed as though the Holy Spirit increased the power flow and he felt as if an even stronger current of electricity was surging through him. There was nothing else for it he had to do it whatever the consequences. Crouching, he crept across the floor behind the seats. He made it to the woman, unobserved by his father. He stood up and said to her, 'I want to pray for you.'

'All right,' she said, 'pray for me.' And there and then the healing ministry of Reinhard Bonnke began.

As he put his hands upon this grown woman it was as if the current of power jolted out of him and into her. Pastor Hermann Bonnke could not help but see. 'Reinhard, what are you doing?'

Seasoned soldiers had trembled at that voice of authority. All eyes in the prayer meeting were now focused on father and son. What had the boy done? Nothing like this had ever happened before in their prayer meeting. Pastor Bonnke, now at the scene, asked the woman, 'What did Reinhard do to you?' She started to shout, 'I've just been healed, I've just been healed. Reinhard put his hands upon me and it was like an electric current that flowed through my body and I am well.' Everybody rejoiced with her.

For Reinhard the experience confirmed his faith in God's healing power, and strengthened his confidence in Christ's continuing ministry of the miraculous. He was both amazed and humbled that God had so used him and was glad that he had obeyed the Holy Spirit's prompting. Remarkably, he has never had a repeat of that sensation of an electric current flowing through his hands. God was teaching him that faith is more important than feeling.

Hermann Bonnke acknowledged that God's hand was upon Reinhard but did not make much show of rejoicing. He accepted that God had made his choice among the sons, and if Reinhard's spiritual progress was a real comfort and encouragement to him, he did not readily reveal his feelings. There is no doubt that he loved his children, but they had never found it easy to understand him. Despite this, the bond between Reinhard and his father grew to the place where they were good friends. Of the six, only Reinhard and his young sister Felicitas continued to follow the Christian path.

However, over thirty years later God showed his mercy in a remarkable way when Jürgen really needed help. As an adult he had mapped out his career and planned his life without God. He had married and for a time he had prospered in his business. As the years passed Reinhard had less and less contact with him. Therefore he was completely unaware that his brother's life had run into real difficulties, that his wife had left him and his best friend had died of cancer. As a result of these and other problems life had lost all meaning for him and he was considering committing suicide.

Deeply depressed, one night Jürgen had a vivid dream in which he was walking on a high bridge when he slipped and fell. He felt himself falling and he cried out, whereupon he awoke with a start to find himself drenched in perspiration.

In his desperate state of mind he knew he should pray, and he found he actually wanted to, but it was so long since he had prayed he didn't know how. A scripture learned in childhood came back to him: 'Call upon me in the day of trouble; I will deliver you' (Psalm 50:15). He got down on his knees and from his heart said, 'Lord, you know that I do not even know that you exist, but my brother Reinhard is your servant. Give me a sign through him that you are alive.'

He had no idea where Reinhard was, but God did. He was fast asleep 6,000 miles away in Africa, oblivious of his brother's prayer and predicament. Suddenly, in the early hours of the morning, Reinhard had a deeply disturbing dream. He also saw a high bridge and his brother walking on it in a kind of fog. There were no guard rails on the bridge and Reinhard was afraid that, shrouded by the mist, his brother might step off the edge. He saw him walk further into the fog. In his dream Reinhard called out his name in desperation. The next sound he heard was a voice crying out from bottomless depths — it was his brother's voice. He awoke to find himself covered in perspiration and he immediately prayed and asked the Lord for understanding.

The Lord answered him that his brother was on the bridge to eternity and that it was Reinhard's responsibility to warn him. He reminded him, 'If you do not warn the godless I will require their blood from your hands.' The fear of God came upon Reinhard and he set about the task of writing to his brother. He did not find it an easy thing to do; in fact he struggled and had to overcome fierce battles in his own heart before getting the letter written. In it he told him about his dream and pleaded with him to accept Jesus Christ as his personal Saviour.

After the letter was written and posted, he was left wondering what might happen. Then just before Christmas, the year was 1987, Reinhard received the most wonderful Christmas present possible: a reply from his brother telling how he had received Jesus as his Saviour. He wrote, 'I am walking with the Lord every day. He has solved all my problems.'

When he read it Reinhard was overcome with emotion and wept for joy. At the same time he trembled to think what would have if he had ignored the God-sent dream and not written. Or if he had penned a different kind of letter.

If only their father had lived to see that day when his son returned to the fold. Although in time Reinhard came to understand his father, he also realised that Hermann had made it harder than it need have been, both for himself and his family. Reinhard resolved that if he married and had children he would do all in his power to express his love for them freely and frequently. But there would be many years yet before he could practise his new principles.

Chapter 5

The Little Missionary

In 1957, when Reinhard was seventeen, the young people in the church at Krempe were enjoying something of a divine visitation of revival power. The blessing was not confined to the youth group but they were the ones at the centre of what was happening. They were praying night and day and the prayer meetings were alive with the presence of God. One or two outsiders were brought to Christ but the move was primarily a renewing of the Christian youth.

Pastor Hermann Bonnke was involved and this was undoubtedly fruit from his years of single-minded commitment to the church. His whole life was given over to prayer, preaching, studying the Bible, and seeking the lost. He had no other agenda. He had always encouraged the scriptural use of the gifts of the Spirit but this was something special. Many of the young people had remarkable, supernatural experiences. God's nearness was awesome.

It was in that atmosphere of faith that Reinhard had a vision of a map of Africa. On it was written very clearly just one place name — Johannesburg. He confesses that at the time his grasp of the geography of Africa was rather vague but one thing bothered him: the city did not appear to be in the right place. In his vision it seemed to be too far south.

At the first opportunity he searched out an atlas. He was impressed when he found that Johannesburg was exactly where it had appeared on his vision map. It confirmed the genuineness of the vision, and the name and location of Johannesburg was thereafter fixed firmly in his mind. Surely this South African city was going to figure in God's plans for his future? It clarified the call to Africa he had received in his childhood.

Seven years earlier during another prayer meeting, a woman in the church shared a vision she had received in which she had seen a white boy 'breaking bread' before thousands of black people. She then turned to Reinhard who was standing by his father and told everyone, 'This is the boy I saw in my vision.'

As a child one of Reinhard's favourite games had been playing at preaching. He and a friend would go into the edge of the nearby forest where no one could see or hear them. Pretending that the trees were people they took it in turn to preach their hearts out, undeterred by their wooden congregation. However, it did seem to Reinhard that his friend was the better preacher and he wondered whether he himself would ever make it to the pulpit. As it transpired, his friend's preaching stint began and ended in the forest. And Reinhard had to wait until he was seventeen for his first real opportunity to preach. But this early interest had earned him the childhood epithet of 'The Little Missionary'.

Shortly after his vision of the map of Africa, the Holy Spirit spoke clearly into Reinhard's heart and said, 'Go to Tostedt and preach there.' As he had not yet begun to preach this was unusual. At the end of the prayer meeting, one of the young people came over to him and said, 'Reinhard, I'm sure that the Holy Spirit spoke to me today and told me we must go and preach the gospel in Tostedt.'

Reinhard was staggered and said to his friend, 'This is from God.'

The immediate confirmation of his own call to preach in Tostedt was electrifying. Tostedt was a town some sixty to sixty-five kilometres south of Krempe, across the river. He sat down there and then and wrote to the pastor in Tostedt, 'The Holy Spirit told us to come and preach in Tostedt.'

That open-hearted man of God wrote back and said, 'You are welcome.' A date was fixed and they saved their pocket money for the train. Reinhard was both excited and nervous. This was his first preaching engagement. He and his friend went 'prayed up and fired up', with all the enthusiasm of youth — after all, had not God told them to go there?

Soon after Reinhard commenced preaching, the Holy Spirit started to work and the whole church began to weep. Afterwards Reinhard felt he was 'on cloud nine'. His preaching ministry had begun and God had graciously blessed his word through him. It was something to remember. Thirty-eight years later, in 1995, a German pastor came up to Reinhard and said, 'Do you remember what happened in Tostedt? I was there and what an occasion that was!'

Nevertheless when he returned home his feet were kept firmly on the ground by a wise pastor who refused to indulge this promising young preacher just because he was his son! Despite their growing relationship, Hermann still did not ask Reinhard to preach in Krempe.

The next year the family home at last moved to Krempe, and Hermann's years of commuting were over. Now his family was with him — at least, Meta his wife, Reinhard and daughter Felicitas, now sixteen, were truly 'with him'. The other sons, Martin aged twenty-four, Gerhard twenty-two, and twins Jürgen and Peter nineteen, were fully intent on going their own ways, having lost all interest in the church, although they remained secure in Hermann's and Meta's hearts and prayers.

The spiritual climate in the Krempe church was good for Reinhard, as was the steadying influence of his parents. Hermann was Pentecostal in practice not just in theory and the manifestation of gifts of the Spirit was taught and encouraged. In consequence these precious gifts were eagerly sought after and appreciated and were regularly in operation by many members of the congregation. The prayer meetings especially

continued to be times of remarkable blessing. Through the gifts
of the Spirit, hidden secrets were revealed with such accuracy
and conviction that fear and trembling fell upon the people. It
was the best commentary possible on Paul's first letter to the
Corinthians, chapters 12, 13 and 14. They did not need anyone
to explain what Paul meant when he wrote, '... if an unbeliever
or someone who does not understand comes in while everybody
is prophesying, he will be convinced by all that he is a sinner and
will be judged by all, and the secrets of his heart will be laid
bare. So he will fall down and worship God exclaiming, "God is
really among you!"' (1 Corinthians 14:24&25). They had seen it
demonstrated and had experienced it for themselves. Reinhard
grew up valuing all the gifts of the Spirit because he had seen
their worth at first hand.

Hermann now knew most certainly that God's hand was
upon Reinhard, as did Meta who had not a few battles with
Reinhard in his teen years. She recognised the strength of his
will, and his resolute determination frightened her at times. So
much so that on one occasion when she was battling with him
over some teenage difference, she said in exasperation, 'I must
break your will.' She did not succeed of course, but no doubt in
the wisdom of God, Meta and Hermann were used to carefully
educate and set that iron will in the only safe direction — the
will of God. Reinhard could hardly wait for the time when he
would be old enough to go to Bible college, but in God's
economy the role of godly parents and the place of the local
church can never be over-estimated.

In 1959, Reinhard was one of a party of some fifty young
people to visit England, at the prompting of an elderly British
preacher, Revd Morris, who had been preaching for Hermann at
Krempe. The war had been over for fourteen years and it was
time to build bridges of friendship. He put them in touch with
Peniel Chapel, a Pentecostal Church in the North Kensington
area of London, noted for its missionary outreach, tract ministry,
aggressive evangelism and open air ministry at Speaker's
Corner, Hyde Park. A second important connection he made for

them was with the People's Church in Liverpool, a charismatic Baptist church pastored by Revd Richard Kayes, where pastor and people were at the vanguard of the new move of the Holy Spirit which was beginning to affect the historic churches in Britain and America.

The coach filled with these eager young German believers took them across to England via the Channel ferry. They had no knowledge of English but they were ready to sing and testify and preach through interpreters. God blessed the trip. People who heard them still remember that there was one in particular who made a lasting impression upon them — a tall, blond-haired young man whose enthusiasm was infectious, called Reinhard.

Equally impressed, Richard Kayes took Reinhard aside and asked him about his future plans. In spite of the language barrier he was able to make it clear that he believed God had called him to preach the gospel in Africa. Richard told him that he knew of a first-class missionary college, the Bible College of Wales in Swansea. It was the first time Reinhard had heard of it but immediately he felt a witness in his heart, as though the Holy Spirit was saying, 'This is the college.'

On returning home, the news that he wanted to apply for admission to the Bible College of Wales was not greeted with any great enthusiasm in the Bonnke household. Hermann knew that the idea of a pastor's son going to a 'foreign Bible college', when their fellowship of Pentecostal churches had a perfectly acceptable Bible college in Germany, would not go down well with his colleagues.

Meta agreed with her husband; it would cause resentment among their friends. She sensed another 'clash of wills' — but Reinhard was adamant. He was absolutely certain in his own heart and mind that this was God's will for him. His single-minded determination has been misunderstood by more than his mother. But from his earliest years as a believer when God has spoken into his heart he has always had the grace to see it through, no matter how great the opposition and how many the disappointments. Once he believes he has heard from God then the issue is settled, it is clear-cut, as straight as an arrow.

Reinhard shared with his parents the way that God had blessed the tour of the young people to Britain and the impression Richard Kayes had made upon him. After discussion and time for prayerful consideration they accepted the situation, and the application was completed and posted to Wales.

While he waited for the reply from Wales, Reinhard was invited to gain experience by working in the Refugee Mission in Berlin. This was 1959, two years before the building of the Berlin Wall. Although Germany was divided into two nations, East and West, it was a time when access to Berlin was still free. But there was a constant stream of refugees from the East into Berlin seeking then to move on into West Germany.

Reinhard prayed about the invitation and felt it was right for him to accept. He had to raise his own support and pay his own fare, and it afforded him his first experience of living by faith. Together with two or three others, he stayed for three invaluable months presenting the gospel to the refugees. It was hard and demanding work but by far the hardest thing he had to bear was a letter from the Bible College of Wales rejecting his application on the grounds that he had no knowledge of the English language. He was stunned. Could he have been mistaken? He prayerfully reconsidered the situation. Other colleges beckoned but he still felt that Wales was the right place for him. He looked to the Lord and waited.

His faith was being tested, but it so happened that while Reinhard was in Berlin, Revd Morris made a second visit to Krempe. He had heard good reports of Reinhard in England, and that he wanted to go to Bible College.

Mr Morris said to Hermann, 'Oh, I know a first class one. It is the Bible College of Wales in Swansea.'

Hermann was impressed that the name should crop up again but had to tell him, 'That is the very college which has turned him down because of his lack of English.'

'Oh no,' said Mr Morris, 'let me write on his behalf. I know the Principal, Samuel Howells. I am sure he will change his mind when I tell him about Reinhard.'

Now they had to wait once more. When the reply came it was favourable — they would accept Reinhard as a student, but he must realise that the lectures and notes were all in English and he would find it difficult.

Reinhard had a glorious three months working at the Refugee Mission in Berlin but it was also a revealing and humbling time for him because he was made to realise his need to gain a fuller and deeper knowledge of the Bible if he was to become an effective evangelist. He left Berlin with a great hunger in his heart to know the word of God and to go to Bible College. When he learned that Mr Morris had written to the college Principal and that he was now accepted, he rejoiced. It was another confirmation that when one is sure of God's leading then doors will always open in God's time and God's way. His faith was strengthened. He knew that it would be very taxing until he gained a working knowledge of English but he was prepared for that.

As expected, the news that the son of Pastor Hermann Bonnke of Krempe was not going to their German Bible College was not well received among their own group of churches. Some were not slow to express themselves.

Reinhard replied, 'It is not a matter of the college not being good enough. I have a call from God for the mission field and I am preparing for it.' The unpleasantness hurt him. Under the confident exterior which some felt bordered on brashness, there was a spirit sensitive to such misunderstandings. Over the years the boldness has increased, but by the grace of God so has the sensitivity of spirit. God the Master Potter takes even more care over the inside of the vessel than over the outside.

Just before Reinhard left for the Bible College of Wales, Hermann gave him his first chance of preaching at Krempe. Reinhard sought God in prayer for the message he should deliver. He was nineteen years of age and about to embark on two years of training to further equip him for his life's calling as a servant of Christ. He felt the Holy Spirit lead him to the passage in Ezekiel where God charged the young prophet that he had made him a watchman to the house of Israel.

Reinhard stood up to preach. He opened his Bible and read the solemn commission that God had given to Ezekiel: 'Son of man, I have made you a watchman for the house of Israel; so hear the word I speak and give them warning from me. When I say to a wicked man, "You will surely die," and you do not warn him or speak out to dissuade him from his evil ways in order to save his life, that wicked man will die for his sin, and I will hold you accountable for his blood'. (Ezekiel 3:17&18).

All eyes were upon him in this church where they had watched him grow over the last ten years from boyhood to manhood. Hermann prayed as he took his seat and prepared to listen to his son preach. He had expected that his eldest son would become the preacher but God had chosen his youngest son. Even so, Hermann was still surprised at the power of Reinhard's preaching.

For forty-five minutes Reinhard poured out his heart. God had called him to be his watchman, warning sinners of their peril. That soul-searching earnestness that marked the beginning of his ministry remains his hallmark to this day. He says, 'The gospel is a confrontation between God and sinners. Don't reduce it to a pleasant introduction. It is not an alternative; it is an ultimatum from the King. "Believe or perish" because "God now commands all men everywhere to repent".'

As Reinhard came to the end of his message, the whole congregation packed into that small church in Krempe began to weep. It was a repetition of what had happened on that memorable day in Tostedt some months before. Afterwards as they gathered around him to wish him well at the Bible College of Wales, they repeated to him and to each other, 'Reinhard you are called by God ... you are called by God.' 'Reinhard is called by God.'

The "Familie Bonnke", Stablack, Germany, 1941.
From left: Meta, Martin, Gerhard, Peter, Jürgen, Hermann, and Reinhard.

The refugee camp in Denmark, Meta Bonnke and children.
(This photo was sent by the Red Cross to Hermann so that he could identify his family. It was to be nearly four years before they were reunited).

Reinhard Bonnke

The young Reinhard. Aged 11. Glückstadt.
Taken by a free-lance photographer when Reinhard was on his way home from Sunday school.

Reinhard's Confirmation, 1953, aged 13. (insisting that he should hold his Bible, he rushed back to get it before the photo could be taken).

1958, a clerical worker in secular employ but, Reinhard continued to feel the call of God upon his life.

Reinhard's first baptism service.

Street meetings during his early days. Every opportunity to preach the gospel was zealously seized.

The musically talented Bonnke family, Krempe 1958.
From left: Peter, Reinhard, Gerhard, Martin, Jürgen, Felicitas,Meta.

Anni & Reinhard. Their wedding day.
20th November 1964. Flensburg.

Wie der Vater mich gesandt hat, so sende ich euch. (Johs. 20/21)

Bitte betet für uns! Eure Missionare Reinhard, Anni u. Kai-Uwe Bonnke
P.O. Box 1636 Johannesburg Süd Afrika

Their first prayer partner card sent out before leaving for Africa, "Please pray for us! Your Missionaries Reinhard, Anni and Kai- Uwe Bonnke"

Leaving for Durban, South Africa, May 1967. Reinhard & Anni with Meta and Hermann. (Note the VW camper-van. This was to be their "mission transport" and whilst on outreach, their accommodation too).

Reinhard would accept to preach at many a funeral even though he did not know the person who had died. Alongside his faithful translator and earliest convert, Dolphin Monese, he would seize every opportunity to minister God's word. "Between bus stops and funerals, it was one way of finding a receptive audience".

Life in Lesotho was full. Anni too would lead ladies meetings and Sunday schools for the local children.

This tent, which held only a few hundred people, was in the early days "massive" yet it was soon be totally inadequate for the crowds, which would come to hear the gospel.It was eventually "shredded by the wind" but it whetted his appetite for tent evangelism.

Gospel meetings and literature distribution in the mountains meant taking to all manner of transport, even bicycle and horseback.

Malawi, 1970. Sometimes he found himself preaching to just five people! ... any more than that was a "revival". (Note the old Mercedes Benz to which he would fit a roof-rack and loudspeaker horns for reaching anticipated "larger" crowds).

Part of the 100-strong Bible Bicycle force that distributed literature to thousands of homes throughout Soweto, South Africa.

As the fore runner to gospel crusades in countries throughout Africa, the African Messenger, sent out by mail in the millions, touched countless thousands of lives.

Over the years Reinhard would minister alongside his trusted colleagues who included Richard Ngidi, Adam Mtsweni, Michael Kolisang and Kenneth Meshoe.

Mafeking 1979. A huge crowd filled the tent and the field around it. The day of the "Combined harvester" had come!

Part of the crowd in the famous Yellow Tent. Up to 10,000 could be crammed in - yet it was also soon to be too small. Potgietersrus, South Africa 1978.

Can it be true?

Cripples walk, the blind receive their sight, deaf ears hear again, the dumb speak, devils are cast out and lives are completely changed. This could not happen, if Jesus was dead, because a dead Christ cannot help anybody. But because He lives, He still works today as in Bible-days. The life of Christ casts out death in all its forms: SIN — FEAR — SICKNESS — DEMON POWER. Convince yourself. Come and experience a Divine miracle in spirit, soul and body.

CAN IT BE TRUE? Oh yes! Countless people all over the world have experienced it. COME, HEAR, SEE, BELIEVE AND RECEIVE — FREELY.

A heap of crutches left behind by p... after JESUS CHRIST H...

I BELONG TO JESUS

Reinhard Bonnke: the Billy Graham of Africa

CHRIST FOR ALL NATIONS

GOSPEL CRUSADE

Come and see God's Miracle Power in Action

with Pastors ... Bonnke ... ...el ...lisane and others

LORD ORDERED A TENT: AND BONNKE WENT OUT AND BUILT THE BIGGEST IN THE WORLD

EVENTH-STOREY HEAVEN

34 000 able to pray in huge gospel tent

THE CITIZEN

Reuse-tent vir sending

Greatest Gospel tent in the world

CFAN erect one of world's tallest mobile structures

From Finland to New Zealand, the international press paid attention to the construction of the "World's Biggest Tent". Raising the masts and setting the huge canopy in position for the first time in December 1982.

he first full campaign in the Big Tent was held in Soweto during February 1984.
housands came to hear the gospel soon packing the "world's largest mobile
tructure" to overflowing. This immense structure which could seat 34,000.
warfed the Yellow Tent which was now only used as a counseling centre for the
ver of new believers.

CfaN CHRIST FOR ALL NATIONS
THE BIG TENT

A year later freak storms destroyed the tent in Cape Town. Five years of toil had
perished in five hours yet God turned this apparent set back into a mighty victory. The
campaign went ahead and the crowds grew to 70,000 - far bigger than the tent could
hold.

CONFERENCE FOR INTERAFRICA · REVIVAL · EVANGELISTS

FIRE

The Big Tent was redesigned and erected alongside the first Fire Conference. With a conference of 4,100 visiting pastors from 41 out of 44 African countries in the mornings and a great gospel crusade in the evenings, Harare, Zimbabwe 1996 was a milestone event.

The campaign trail headed northwards to Malawi where Reinhard was invited to speak to a special session of the House of Parliament.

The Malawi Miracle, Blantyre, 1996. The final gathering was in the region of 150,000 and the number of responses for salvation was phenomenal. The ministry had outgrown even the Big Tent and open air events would now be the format.

Evangelist Reinhard Bonnke and his wife Anni

Frankfurt, Germany, 1986. The New Christ for all Nations Headquarters.

Great Expectations

The guard blew his whistle and waved his green flag, and the train bearing Reinhard on the first leg of his journey to Bible College quickly picked up speed, leaving Hermann and Meta waving their tearful farewells on the station platform. Reinhard leaned out of the carriage window and waved back to them as he watched them grow smaller with every chug of the engine, until they disappeared from view.

He wound up the window and took his seat on the train. For the tenth time he checked his tickets, train connections, ferry connection across the Channel. Even though he had been to England on the Youth Tour this was very different. Then there were fifty of them and they were home in two weeks; now he was on his own and it might be two years before he saw his home again. The journey from north Germany to Wales seemed like going to the ends of the earth. Yet he knew he was not alone and he was excited at the prospect of studying at the Bible College of Wales in Swansea.

His travel-tiredness was quickly forgotten when he caught his first glimpse of the college buildings. He was in Wales, the land of revivals, and this college, founded by the outstanding man of prayer and faith, Rees Howells, had an international reputation for its missionary vision. His friends Revd Morris and Richard Kayes had told him stories about Rees Howells and the college, including many marvellous answers to prayer, as well as a college faculty who chose to 'live by faith' — refusing a regular salary and trusting God to supply their needs.

He did not need to understand English to appreciate the warmth of the welcome he received from the staff and students. They were kind and considerate and in spite of the language barrier (his knowledge of English was almost nil) he quickly felt at home. He had a reassuring witness in his heart that this was the right place for him.

Most of the students were from Britain, but he soon found that there were other foreign students, including French, Dutch, and an Arab. He also discovered that although the college faculty 'lived by faith', most of them were highly qualified and dedicated teachers who did not believe in sparing themselves or their students. They believed in academic excellence and the only way to achieve that was by studying and working hard.

The foreign students were put in a separate class where mastery of English was the main goal. All the students, including those from Britain, were tested on their knowledge of the English language and a few British students whose written English was not good enough also found themselves in this special class. For three months, under the unsparing tuition of a Dr Symonds, Reinhard's group was subjected to intensive teaching of English with strict attention to grammar, grammar and more grammar.

It paid off and Reinhard is for ever grateful for the solid grounding he received. Dr Symonds was an excellent teacher and Reinhard was a willing student. Even so he was shocked when at the end of the three months Dr Symonds told him that he had arranged his first preaching engagement. It was to be in a few days' time, in a church not too far away in the Welsh Valleys, and he must preach in English without an interpreter.

Reinhard prayed hard and prepared diligently but it seemed a well-nigh impossible assignment. The day came almost too quickly for him. But he threw himself on the mercy of God and found a flow of words coming, and that precious anointing of God's Spirit which he had experienced in Tostedt and Krempe came upon him again. Welsh people are a people of the Spirit and readily respond when a preacher is inspired. When he finished preaching, the people found it hard to believe that it was only three months since he had arrived from Germany with virtually no English, and they took him to their hearts. Further preaching opportunities followed as Dr Symonds made engagements over as many weekends as possible.

The first-year students were also sent on a regular basis to preach to the patients at the Mount Pleasant psychiatric hospital. Reinhard and his fellow students found even their most fervent preaching met with blank stares. Dr Symonds clearly possessed a wry sense of humour. Reinhard preached there many times and it was a testing but most effective training ground which he still remembers with a smile.

His ability to preach so fluently in English continues to amaze those who hear him. This was one of several benefits he gained from the college, the full significance of which would become apparent only in the future. Today he has preached far more in English than in German. But God knew that beforehand and his guidance proved to be right.

Reinhard found himself sharing a room with a second-year student called Bryn Jones, the only other student from a Pentecostal background. He was bright, forceful, outgoing and Welsh, an explosive combination. Like Reinhard, Bryn was also showing promise as a fiery evangelist, but being of different years and languages, they never became close friends. However, despite doctrinal differences, their roots enabled them to encourage each other, for although the college was interdenominational, Pentecostalism was by no means fully accepted. The first wave of the charismatic renewal was only just beginning to lap the shores of the historic churches.

Every stone of the extensive college buildings was a testimony to the faith of Rees Howells. Shortly after returning home from missionary service with the South African General

Mission, God directed him to establish a Bible College for training young people for the mission field. When Rees and his wife Elizabeth knelt on a Welsh mountain to dedicate themselves to the task, they had less than a pound between them. In 1923 he came across a mansion overlooking Swansea Bay and an inner voice witnessed, 'This is the college.' He prayed in the thousands of pounds needed and the college opened on Whit Monday, 1924.

In 1930, a neighbouring property was secured for the expanding college and once again the thousands of pounds needed were prayed in. In 1932 God challenged him to open a school for the children of missionaries. Another adjoining property was obtained, the money prayed in, and the school opened in 1933. Beginning with less than one pound, in fourteen years he had prayed for and received £125,000. It was an epic of faith with the money usually coming in at the last moment.

After the founder of the college, Rees Howells, had died in 1950, his son Samuel Howells carried on the faith traditions of his father. This 'living by faith' intrigued Reinhard. It permeated every aspect of the college life. All the staff, cook and lecturer alike, received food and board but had to believe God to supply the extras. It was a constant demonstration to the students of the power of faith. One of the rules was that no appeals were to be made known except to God, and the students were encouraged to prove for themselves that God does answer prayer. A phrase in constant use by the staff was, 'I've been delivered,' which Reinhard soon learned signified that the person had received the answer to their prayer.

One morning, Principal Samuel Howells came into the room where the students were gathered for a prayer meeting and invited them to pray with him for a sum of several hundred pounds which was needed by the end of the week to pay the fuel bill for the extensive college buildings. He reminded them that this was solely a matter for prayer and that no financial appeals were to be made. Reinhard was keenly interested in seeing the outcome, for it was a large sum of money and was required within a short and fixed period of time.

At the end of the week when the students were again gathered for prayer, Samuel Howells came in and with shining eyes he announced, 'Praise God, we've been delivered!' They all rejoiced. Reinhard's spirit responded, 'Lord, I want to be a man of faith.'

The reality of his desire was soon put to the test. He had come to college with good support financially from his parents and the church, and friends in Germany sent him parcels and money for his various needs. As he prayed he felt that God was challenging him to 'give away all the money he had'; furthermore, 'he was to give it to a missionary who would be visiting the college'. He accepted the challenge but decided that it would be circumspect of him to keep back one pound — just in case an emergency should arise. No sooner had he done this than he knew that it was the wrong decision and God rebuked him for this 'natural wisdom'. It was nothing less than a disguise for unbelief which would not give God the full chance to work a miracle for him. He realised that it had to be all or nothing and sensed that the decision would have life-forming repercussions one way or another.

It did not take him long to decide; it had to be all. It was the launching pad into the realm of faith for finance. He little realised that the day would come when he would be able to trust God to supply millions of pounds at short notice and with no emergency fund.

The missionary came and the money duly went — all of it. It was a new experience for Reinhard. Mercifully, God starts us off with small things. In Reinhard's case it was a postage stamp. How he prayed and how he rejoiced when his prayer was answered. Never was a stamp pressed on an envelope with so much praise to God!

Next the 'new student in the faith' found himself required to graduate from a postage stamp to a bus ticket, or two tickets to be precise. He was assigned to speak at a special gospel service for children, on one of the beaches in Swansea popularly known as 'Sunshine Corner'. It attracted scores of children and their parents, and under the blessing of God many had come to know Christ as their Saviour.

It was a bus ride away from the college. After the stamp episode Reinhard had also received a small amount of money. On the day in question he had just half-a-crown, which was the cost of a return ticket for one. But Reinhard had become friends with a Dutch student called Tuinis, and he asked him to accompany him. Tuinis said he would love to but could not because he was out of funds. Reinhard told him he had enough for two single tickets. Fine, but Tuinis wanted to know how they would get back. 'Let's trust God to get us back,' responded Reinhard. One postage stamp had given his faith an amazing lift!

It was a beautiful sunny day and they enjoyed everything, the bus ride, the children's meeting, the stroll on the beach afterwards. Now came the test — two bus tickets back to the college. How would God supply the need? Reinhard prayed, in German, in English and in tongues. Suddenly among the crowds Reinhard spotted a familiar face, a local pastor known to both of them. Surely this was the answer to his prayer.

Their hopes were high when the pastor responded to their over-eager greetings by inviting them to join him for afternoon tea in a restaurant overlooking the beach. Reinhard felt confident, for surely God had arranged this happy meeting. They enjoyed listening to the stories of his experiences in serving God. Reinhard then tried to hurry things along by telling the pastor that they would have to leave in a moment to catch their bus. God's servant paid the bill, thanked them for their fellowship, and shook their hands most warmly ... but they left empty-handed.

Reinhard's faith was tested and so was Tuinis' patience. 'What was it you said? "Let's see what God can do for us." Now what do we do?'

Reinhard searched his heart. Had he been presumptuous to invite Tuinis? No, he still felt he had done the right thing. He hung on bravely, trying not to give in to doubt.

Then suddenly he heard the sound of heavy breathing and hurrying footsteps. They both turned to see an elderly lady almost running towards them. She gasped out, 'Boys, I enjoyed so much the Sunshine Corner meeting on the beach this afternoon. Here, please accept this,' and she thrust two coins into Reinhard's hand. When he looked and found they were two half-crowns he could hardly contain his joy.

'Hallelujah ... look Tuinis ... we are delivered!' Faith had just moved from the future tense to the present tense.

'Thank you, thank you, God bless you,' they enthused as they boarded the bus, and they waved to her with happy abandon as the bus moved away.

At the bus stop their unlikely deliverer gazed after them, still gasping for breath, unaware of the full significance of the role she had played in helping to establish those boys on the path of a faith which one day would be able to believe God for the funds to take the gospel of Christ to the ends of the earth.

Reinhard was now firmly enrolled in God's school of faith and he was a quick and discerning learner. He realised it had been a mistake to look to the pastor just because he seemed to be the kind of deliverer one would expect. And even worse had been the way he had tried to hurry things along in the restaurant when time seemed to be running out. Deliverance had come in time, even though it had arrived at the last minute and from a most unexpected source. But it had come. He was learning that faith believes that God is always on time and looks to God alone, leaving the choice of deliverer to him.

Reinhard had settled well into the routine of college life. Even in a place as famous for faith as this was, dramatic answers to prayer were not happening every day. He applied himself to his studies, and the discipline of regular lectures and the daily contact with keen students of other persuasions and nationalities combined to aid the maturing of his personality and the enriching of his character.

The months flew by and the time was quickly approaching for the end of another term. As he was praying he felt that it would be right for him to go home to Germany during the college recess. He had no money for the fare but his faith had now arrived at a place where he believed he could trust God to provide. So confident was he that he went into Swansea, found a travel agent, and made the necessary booking. The cost was considerable but fortunately no deposit was demanded. Once back at the college Reinhard began to pray in real earnest for the money he now needed. Booking 'in faith' was easy but praying in this kind of money was a different proposition altogether. It certainly succeeded in putting a new urgency into his praying which increased dramatically when, two or three days before the departure date, a phone call from the travel agency informed him that they had received his ticket and would he kindly call in and collect it and, of course, pay for it.

Reinhard had told no one. He had learned that living by faith demanded that it was kept between him and God. One day remained. He prayed fervently and looked eagerly for a letter which might bring him the desperately needed deliverance. The day for his departure dawned and sure enough there was a letter for him but his hopes were dashed when he found it contained only a circular. The pressure increased with another phone call from the travel agency reminding him that his ticket still had not been collected and his train would be leaving shortly after noon.

Reinhard needed no reminding. But he assured the travel agent he would be collecting it.

His friend Tuinis found him on his knees. Reinhard invited his friend to pray with him. Reinhard's bags were packed; everything was there except the money. After a short time of apparently fruitless praying, he suggested to his friend that they should go into one of the empty classrooms where they could pray without restraint. The volume of their praying increased by several decibels. If praying depended on the loudness of their cries, heaven must surely have heard! But the heavens remained as brass.

The situation was desperate. Then the words of a chorus came to mind and he started to sing, 'There's nothing too hard for Thee ... I'm trusting alone in Thee ... It's never too late for Thee dear Lord.' As they were singing the last verse something happened in his heart. He suddenly knew that God had answered. He could not explain it, but there was an inner certainty, and he believed it. Tuinis was startled when Reinhard stood up and shouted, 'The money is there!'

Tuinis asked, 'Where?'

And Reinhard answered with a confidence which amazed even himself, his faith having somehow laid hold of the unseen, 'I don't know, but I know it is there!'

Together they left the classroom and raced across the garden on their way back to their rooms. Turning round one of the hedges they ran into Tim, a fellow student. Like them he was a little out of breath from hurrying. He looked at Reinhard and asked, 'How much money do you need?' It would have been so easy to tell him but Reinhard instinctively knew that would not be consistent with faith and he replied, 'God knows the amount. I'm not telling you.'

Tim put his hand in his pocket, pulled out a handful of money, gave it to Reinhard and turned and left them without another word. Astonished and rejoicing Reinhard counted it and Tuinis checked it. It was the amount needed for the fare. What an answer to prayer!

With time enough but none to spare, Reinhard said farewell to Tuinis, grabbed his bags and dashed off into Swansea to collect his ticket. He just made his train and all the way home he rejoiced. He had proved God for himself. He had moved into a new realm of faith.

After the break at home, he settled down again to his studies, knowing that God had more lessons to teach him at Swansea. The only way to master God's word was by 'studying to show themselves approved unto God, workmen that needed not to be ashamed'. He applied himself diligently to the task but it was hard work. Even though he had amazed himself as well as his hearers at the success of his first effort at preaching in English, he knew that while God had helped him, he still had to help himself. Often he would stay up late transcribing notes from English into German, and vice versa. It was all valuable experience, however, and laid the foundation of his ability for sound, concentrated study, which has never deserted him.

Of the lecturers, one above all really blessed Reinhard. Iewan Jones had been at the college from the days of Rees Howells, and was now an elderly man. Reinhard had come to Wales with the burning desire in his heart to learn how to 'correctly handle the word of truth'. He knew that if ever he was to become a really successful evangelist it was vital for him to know and understand the Bible from cover to cover. As he sat at the feet of Iewan Jones he was thrilled.

Never before had he heard the word of God so beautifully and wonderfully expounded. He drank deeply from the wisdom of this skilful man of God. Iewan was Calvinistic in his theology, but Reinhard learned to take the fish without choking on the bones. It is this ability to appreciate others of differing viewpoints which has enabled him to keep forging straight ahead in his quest for souls while avoiding the many diversions that lead nowhere.

From boyhood he had been an avid reader of the lives of missionaries. His two years in Wales had increased his appreciation for the great pioneers of the faith, such as David Livingstone, and he longed to follow in his footsteps. Africa burned in his heart, and the name Johannesburg continued to ring loud and clear in his ears. At the same time, he had an increased urgency to reach the lost in these last days, when God was pouring out his Spirit on all flesh. He set his face for home with a heart open for all God had for him.

On the way God had a surprise for him, the full significance of which did not really hit him until he had been in Africa for a number of years.

The Watchmen of
the Night

The train from Swansea took Reinhard Bonnke to London where he had a few hours to spare before the next stage of his journey to the overnight ferry. He was told the time-honoured way of seeing London was by the world-famous, red London buses. Having enough money for a run-about ticket, he travelled the streets of the capital, changing buses at random. He was free, he was going home, and life and London looked wonderful from the top deck of a double-decker bus.

After an hour or two he needed exercise, so he alighted at the next stop and strolled down the road, with little idea where he was except that he was still within the bus routes of London. As he enjoyed the walk, a sign informed him that this area was called Clapham. The name meant nothing to him and he walked on until he found himself outside a house with a wooden fence around it and on it a board bearing the name, Principal George Jeffreys. He stopped in his tracks and looked at the name again. It was there clear enough, but no; he dismissed it, it could not be.

Only a few weeks earlier, he had been browsing through the books in the college library when he chanced upon *Healing Rays* by George Jeffreys. His interest was quickly aroused as he scanned through the contents. It was a balanced scriptural exposition on the subject of divine healing. The final chapter was full of testimonies of miracles in the ministry of George Jeffreys which were witnessed by huge congregations in the largest halls throughout the British Isles. The founder and leader of the Elim Foursquare Gospel Alliance, he had clearly been a greatly anointed evangelist.

Reinhard had been absorbed, but he noted that the miracles mostly occurred in the 1920s. He presumed that this great evangelist must be dead, and when he had left college, George Jeffreys had been far from his thoughts.

But now he wondered. Was it possible that this great evangelist was still alive and lived here? He had almost decided that it was nonsense even to think so, when the Holy Spirit seemed to whisper in his heart, 'Why don't you find out?'

Contrary to what people may think when they see him in action on a platform, Reinhard is not one to rush into things; he likes to think before he acts. But at once he knew he must know the truth.

He went up to the front door and rang the bell. Just when he was beginning to think that there was no one in, a woman opened the door.

'Excuse me,' he asked, 'but I saw the nameplate and wondered, is this the home of George Jeffreys the mighty evangelist who reached a whole nation?'

'Yes it is the same man,' she replied.

'Please, do you think that I may see him? I have just finished at Bible college and I am on my way home to Germany.'

Her reply was an unpromising 'No', and with that she started to close the door, when a voice echoed from within, 'Let him come in.'

In went the wondering Reinhard and there, coming down the stairs, was the frail figure of an elderly man. In a deep husky voice, he greeted Reinhard and asked him what he wanted. Reinhard explained how he had just finished Bible College and the call of God was on his life to be a missionary in Africa.

He was led into one of the rooms, and invited to sit down. George Jeffreys sat down opposite him on a couch and began to ask Reinhard lots of questions about himself. The fact that Reinhard had been at college in Wales helped to open the conversation with this Welsh preacher whose roots were in the Great Revival there in 1904, and the conversation ignited with the fire of a spiritual rapport which obliterated the generation gap. It was a meeting of two kindred souls with a mutual passion for evangelism. One who was reckoned by many to be the greatest British evangelist of this century, who knew he was coming to the end of his life. The other an eager young man who knew that God had given him the ministry of an evangelist, taking up the mantle of his ministry.

Suddenly the old man slid onto his knees, pulling Reinhard down with him. The glory of God came on Reinhard as George Jeffreys laid his hands upon his head and prayed for him. The tired but still eloquent voice gained in strength as the old Welsh revivalist poured out his soul in prayer for the raw and eager young man whom God had brought to his house for him to bless. He who had spent his life beseeching sinners to receive Christ was again seeking the face of God for the lost, but through the ministry of this young German kneeling with him.

Did God give George Jeffreys a glimpse into the future ministry of Reinhard Bonnke? Was he allowed a foresight of the tremendous expansion of the revival which was just at hand? We cannot know, but when Reinhard finally rose from his knees he knew that he had received something powerful from God. He left the house 'dazed' at what had happened as the house-keeper closed the door behind him.

He could not take it all in. He had not even had George Jeffreys on his mind, yet in a city of around ten million people God had brought him to the man's door. The more he thought about it the more he thanked God for so leading him. He caught the night train for the Channel ferry and travelled back via Belgium to his home in Germany. Hermann and Meta were so glad to have their son home again and they all had much to talk about, but Reinhard did not mention his meeting with the great evangelist.

A few weeks later, Hermann said, 'Reinhard, I have just received news that George Jeffreys, the famous evangelist, has died.'

Reinhard was stunned. 'That cannot be, surely? I saw him a few weeks ago on my way home.' Then he shared with his father the story of that wonderful meeting. In the light of the great man's death the encounter was seen to be even more remarkable.

Twenty-five years later, in August 1986, Reinhard Bonnke conducted a campaign in Blantyre, Malawi, named after the birthplace in Scotland of David Livingstone, the great Africa missionary explorer. God so owned the ministry of his servant that by the closing service, the crowds attending had grown to over 150,000. Later on in the year another campaign followed in Lilongwe, and again many thousands came to hear the gospel message. It was during this time that Reinhard was deeply moved by certain stirring words written by David Livingstone over a century before in 1853 when in that same region:

> Future missionaries will be rewarded by conversions for every sermon. We are their pioneers and helpers. Let them not forget the watchmen of the night, we who worked when all was gloom and no evidence of success in the way of conversion cheered our path. They will doubtless have more light than we, but we served our Master earnestly and proclaimed the same gospel as they will do.

More than once as Reinhard blazed across Africa, the Holy Spirit reminded him of the immeasurable debt he owed to the many 'watchmen of the night' in whose steps he was treading. Most of them like Livingstone were long dead, but as Scripture says of Abel, they 'by faith still speak'. However, in the providence of God he had been allowed to meet one or two special watchmen of the twentieth century.

It was not until he was praying about the momentous decision to move the centre of his operations from Africa to Frankfurt in Germany that the Holy Spirit brought it very specially to his attention. Suddenly everything connected. God gave him a new realisation about how we build on the people who have gone before us, those watchmen who faithfully carried the torch of truth in their generation, defied the darkness, and handed on the baton to those coming after who were ready to respond to the call of God; people such as David Livingstone, Rees Howells and George Jeffreys, and he knew that in some way God had helped him to grasp a baton. The greatness of the responsibility weighed heavily upon him. He must not fail.

The more he thought back over that meeting with George Jeffreys the more he realised how God had planned it; not only the amazing timing of it, so close to the end of the evangelist's life; not only as a German whose nation had been at war with Britain only a few years before; not only on the day he had finished at college; but also with one of the greatest evangelists of this century. God had confirmed his calling and this special experience seemed to cover him with an added mantling of his power.

Considering the incident under the direction of the Holy Spirit strengthened him and caused him to thank God for his guidance, but he was also enabled to keep it all in perspective. He knew that even the great George Jeffreys had made mistakes which had almost certainly limited his effectiveness in his later years. Nothing could ever detract from what the evangelist had achieved, but sadly he had become involved in a dispute over church government which ultimately caused division in the Elim movement, and had also been taken up with another unprofitable diversion which led nowhere except to more controversy. It was a sombre lesson. If so great a man could make mistakes which marred his ministry, then what hopes for him? He prayed that God would continue to direct his paths and deliver him from ever being diverted from evangelism.

None of God's servants is superhuman, and Reinhard is aware that one day people may gloat over his mistakes also. We are what we are by the grace of God. An incident which could easily have puffed him up has served to keep him humbly aware of his need to watch and pray. The path of a successful evangelist is full of pit falls.

Recognition and Romance

Not long after Reinhard's return home in 1961, after completing his two years at Bible College, one of the German leaders made it his business to inform him, 'You know we do not recognise that college — you will still have to come to us,' meaning the German Bible College. Reinhard was staggered at this statement, but not too staggered to respond, 'I will not.'

Happily, six months later the same leader came to him again and humbly admitted, 'Reinhard, we have watched you and we will recognise the Welsh Bible College and fully accept your course there.' He was greatly relieved because he valued the German Pentecostal Fellowship (BFP) and wanted to keep a good relationship with them. They saw that the anointing of God's Spirit was upon his life and ministry and that was the validation they recognised. Reinhard says he has found that this ability to recognise the anointing upon someone's life and ministry is common to Spirit-filled men in every part of the world.

The call to Africa never left him but he was only twenty-one years old and he knew that Hudson Taylor, the great China missionary, was right when he said, 'Crossing the sea never made a missionary.' First he must prove his calling in his homeland of Germany. It was not long before he began to receive invitations and opportunities for ministry, but which should he accept? Hermann had never indulged Reinhard because he was his son; rather the opposite, lest he should ever be accused of nepotism. But Hermann had more than enough proof to know that God had called his youngest son and he recognised that God was giving him a chance to help Reinhard at the beginning of his ministry.

So Hermann invited Reinhard to come and work with him in his church, giving him all the liberty he needed, both in preaching in the various out-stations of his church and for evangelism of all kinds. Soon Reinhard was away for four or five weeks at a time. It was especially significant that it was not long before he was conducting evangelistic missions in gospel tents. He little dreamed that the day would come when he would launch a whole new concept of evangelism with the world's biggest tent in South Africa.

That day was a long way off and in 1962 an invitation to conduct his first major evangelistic campaign in a tent really scared him. It was not the size of the tent that worried him but the length of the campaign — three whole weeks. The invitation had come about when he had gone with Hermann to Rendsburg for a meeting of the pastors in the region. The local pastor, quite an old man, came to him and said, 'I would like to invite you to have a three-week tent campaign here in Rendsburg. I have prayed about it and the Lord has told me you are the one.'

Reinhard was nervous of accepting due to one reason: he did not have twenty-one different evangelistic sermons! So he replied, 'That is impossible. Perhaps a year later. I feel it is too much for me now.' The old pastor looked at this tall stripling and said, 'The Lord spoke to me.' And the trembling stripling replied, 'Then the Lord will speak to me.' He went home and prayed about it, and as he did he felt the Lord speaking into his heart through the story of the feeding of the five thousand: 'Go, and twelve baskets full will remain.' He informed the pastor of his acceptance.

The weeks flew by and the day for the beginning of the tent campaign was all too suddenly upon an apprehensive Reinhard. He packed his little Volkswagen car in good time, and set off for Rendsburg. He was so anxious not to be late for this his first real evangelistic campaign that he arrived hours early. He drove to the site where the tent was pitched and ventured inside to explore. He found a woman there whom he did not know and after greeting her he asked, 'Are you expecting many people?'

She replied, 'You know there is supposed to be a very young evangelist coming but the church elders are all against it. The pastor did it entirely on his own and we don't know what to expect.'

The heart of the very young evangelist sank to rock bottom. He took his leave of this female descendant of Job's comforters, and drove out into the countryside until he found a deserted place. He switched off the car engine and in desperation he cried out to the Lord, 'Oh God, have mercy on me. Here I have come, already with much trembling, only to find that the people don't even expect anything. I feel trapped.' He stayed there as long as possible, praying, until he knew he must leave and drive to the tent.

The pastor called him to the platform and introduced him to the congregation. Reinhard could not resist looking around the tent for one particular person, and sure enough there she was — hiding her face in embarrassment now she knew the identity of the young man she had talked to earlier!

He preached every day for three weeks and God was with him from the very outset. The church members took him to their hearts and the Spirit of God moved with power. Many were won to Christ and gloriously saved and changed; many sick people were healed and delivered. One woman in particular was healed and delivered from demonic oppression and over thirty-five years later she was still sending a monthly missionary offering to support Reinhard's ministry.

The last service saw the tent full and the campaign had created such a stir in Rendsburg that the newspaper sent one of their reporters to interview the evangelist. When Reinhard came to speak with him he said, 'No, no, I don't want to talk to the tent deacon, I want to talk to the evangelist himself.' Reinhard had quite a job persuading this hardened reporter that he was the evangelist responsible, under God, for creating so much interest. He had only just turned twenty-two years of age and he had long had to cope with the embarrassment of looking much younger than he actually was. He was tall and well-built, but he had only just started shaving!

As he was leaving, the pastor came to him and said, 'I have had big name evangelists here but I have never had such a move of God. He will use you in your life as you never thought possible. I see God's hand on you as I have never seen on anybody else.' The faith of the old pastor in inviting Reinhard had been justified. He had taken a risk, but it has been well said, 'Faith is spelt, R-I-S-K.'

The campaign which had commenced so unpromisingly for the 'unknown young evangelist' ended with the promise of greater things to come. Some of the new believers were so thrilled at entering into the experience of salvation through Christ that they arranged a special visit to his father's church in Krempe where they testified with tears of joy how God had transformed their lives. Hermann rejoiced with them and with Reinhard, whose ministry as an evangelist began to develop rapidly from that time. The Rendsburg campaign proved to be very formative for him. True to the promise which God had given him, he found that instead of running out of sermons he was left with twelve baskets full of gospel truths to develop for the future.

While he was based at the Krempe church under Hermann he received 50DM a month (five pounds). Hermann and Meta were to provide his food and board, and once a year the church was to buy him a new suit. It was very basic, but he had learned the lessons of faith and he found that enough support came in for his needs. He was being grounded in the correct handling of money as a servant of Christ, and over those formative years financial integrity became second nature to him.

Money and women have proved the undoing of more than one evangelist. Reinhard remembered the untold damage that had been done to the cause of Christ when the American evangelist, under whose ministry Hermann had been healed and saved, was guilty of a moral lapse. He had also seen the harm done by some of his friends who were careless in their relationships. But Reinhard knew that he may well have to preach to some of these girls. As a man called by God he must be above reproach.

There was one girl in the church youth group whom he liked but he had never made any approach to her. He watched her and wondered if she was the one. The call to Africa was still uppermost in his heart and he knew that if ever he did find a wife she must be willing to go to Africa. He kept his feelings to himself but waited for a suitable opportunity to arise. The chance came and he fell into conversation with her. As casually as possible he asked her, 'If God called you to Africa, would you go?' Her response was prompt and emphatic, 'Never, never in my life. I would never leave Germany.' That was it, end of conversation and end of any further interest in the girl.

However, not long after this he was attending a youth conference in the area. A group of young people from another church provided a singing item under the leadership of a young woman who also accompanied them on a mandolin. They started singing but the song had been pitched too high and soon they were in difficulty. They just could not reach the top notes. Without any fuss the young woman on the mandolin stopped them and with an engaging smile and a pleasant little chuckle said, 'Oh, we have got the wrong pitch. we'll start again,' and they did. Her composure and natural charm turned an embarrassing situation into a blessing and for Reinhard it was a case of 'love at first sight'. He was smitten — he could not take his eyes off this bright and attractive girl. His heart was thumping, as though he had been struck by lightning. He discovered that her name was Anni Sülzle, but she was oblivious of the stir she had caused in his heart, and he knew he dare not pursue his interest in her until he found out whether she would be willing to go to Africa.

Being cautious and very shy, his first contact with her was through others. He was overjoyed when he discovered that she had a separate call to the mission field. Once he had made this all- important discovery he wrote to her. Although he had never heard of her before, she knew of his growing reputation as a young evangelist. It was not long before they were exchanging letters.

Anni came from a large, well brought-up family of eight children. They were country folk, and like Reinhard had come through severe privations during and after the war. She had actually been born in Romania, but the family had returned to north Germany in 1949. They kept an open house, always full of guests, and meal times were always thronged with young people.

She had become a Christian at the local Sunday school, and from an early age wanted to train as a nurse so that she could go to the mission field. Meanwhile, determined to acquire skills, she taught herself shorthand and typing, and learned the mandolin. She had always dreamed of marrying a missionary, and her friendship with Reinhard quickly blossomed!

After the Rendsburg campaign Reinhard was kept very busy conducting evangelistic campaigns and preaching. Within two years the BFP, the German Pentecostal Fellowship of Churches, told him that they were now ready to ordain him as one of their ministers. Reinhard felt that this was the time for him to launch out and establish his own ministry in preparation for the day when he would leave for Africa. He learned that there was a small city called Flemsburg in the north of Germany, situated on the border with Denmark, which had no Pentecostal church. He organised a team of young people, borrowed a tent, and planned a pioneer campaign with a view to planting a church there.

The campaign was planned to last for six weeks. A friend would preach the first three weeks, and he the last three. He did not know a single person in that place before the campaign. With Hermann's and Meta's blessing he knew that this was the time for him to leave home, and in 1964 he moved to Flemsburg before the campaign commenced. The campaign was a success; people were saved and healed and a lot of interest was aroused. They finished with a nucleus of fifty people (many of them new believers) who were definitely interested in becoming part of a new church. In the context of the 1960s in Germany it was an excellent start.

The next problem was to find suitable premises for the fledgling church, but although he searched, he could find nothing. Finally, in despair, he prayed, 'Lord you must show me where,' and then drove his Volkswagen around Flemsburg, praying as he went. Among other things the city had been famous as a centre of the rum-making trade. He passed an old five-storey building which was shuttered up and empty, but it was a good site in the centre and he felt he should investigate. Reinhard found an open door and climbed the stairs to a flat on the top floor occupied by someone who could answer his questions.

The premises, which used to be the headquarters of a rum factory, had been vacated prior to demolition to make way for a new shopping centre. This, however, was probably not going to happen for a year or so, and the agent handling it was located some thirty miles away. With a sense of expectation he drove off to find the agent who turned out to be a man in a wheelchair. The course of the conversation quickly switched to the most important subject in the world — Jesus and salvation. Afterwards the agent told him he could use the building during the interim period before the demolition and then asked, 'How much rent can you pay?'

With brutal frankness Reinhard replied, 'Very little!' To his joy and astonishment a ridiculously low rent was agreed, whereupon he asked, 'How much shall I have to pay for heating?' He could hardly believe his ears when the agent told him, 'Oh the heating is on anyway so that is included in the rent.'

God had obviously given him favour with this man. The contract was signed and with lots of willing help in cleaning and painting they were able to move in after the end of the tent campaign.

It turned out to be an excellent place for the follow-up meetings and under Reinhard's enthusiastic leadership the new church prospered and increased. It was a vital period of learning in his training as an international evangelist. He proved for himself the difficulties and care needed to establish new believers in the Christian faith. The expertise called for in follow-up work has stayed with him and in his campaigns he devotes as much energy and effort to the after-care of new believers as in bringing them to initial trust in Christ.

In spite of leading a very busy life he made time for his friendship and love for Anni to grow stronger and deeper. God had honoured his integrity and given him a woman after his own heart. Her call to serve overseas was as real as his and although tempting offers were made to them to stay in Germany, they both knew that their future lay in Africa. They also agreed that the time was right for them to marry and two months after the new church moved into the building they were married.

Reinhard and Anni decided that they should be married where their first home would be, in Flemsburg. What a day that turned out to be for all concerned: the two families, the Bonnkes and Sülzles; their many friends; and especially the members of the new church. Hermann officiated at the wedding service which took place on the 20th November 1964. God had brought him and his family through incredibly difficult times. How good

God had been to him to free him from the army and make him a pastor and his youngest son an evangelist.

Reinhard and Anni revelled in being together and how they enjoyed those precious first two years in Flemsburg, seeing God work through them to build up the newly planted church.

Anni turned her hand to whatever came her way, often finding herself cooking for thirty people without notice, or once, soon after they were married, packing Reinhard's case for him. She has done it ever since, although that first time she forgot his razor and his socks!

But Africa was calling and before long they applied to the Velberter Mission, the Foreign Mission arm of BFP.

When the mission board interviewed Reinhard they asked him which part of Africa he felt called to.

'South Africa,' he replied.

'We don't send missionaries to South Africa,' they said, wanting him to work in Zambia. But Reinhard could not and would not deny God's directions in his life. The call to Africa had come when he was only a boy and had been confirmed independently. The vision of the map of Africa and the name of Johannesburg had never left him. He believed that God had spoken to him and all the efforts of the august members of the mission board could not persuade him otherwise. In his own words, 'I stuck to my guns like crazy' and in the end they miraculously agreed to send him to South Africa with the proviso that he should look around and take a year to decide.

Meanwhile he and Anni were asked to undertake deputation work to make themselves and the work in Africa known among the German churches. And so it was that in 1966 they prepared to hand over the pastorate of the work at Flemsburg to their

successor. It was a place and a time in their lives they would
never forget.

Before they left they had another cause for celebration — the
birth of their first child, a son, Kai-Uwe Friedrich Bonnke, in
1966. The following year, after busy months of deputation work
amongst the churches, interspersed with seemingly endless
preparations for the move to Africa, they were ready. Their
passages were booked, and early in 1967 the young family set
sail for Durban in South Africa.

Part Two

The Mission Field

Chapter 9

Africa: A Tough Start

From the deck of the ocean liner, the little groups of people who had come to see the vessel off looked small and forlorn under the towering gantries which lined the dock like a row of iron giants. The huge vessel moved slowly away from the dockside with deafening blasts of her horns as those around them strained to get a last glimpse of their friends and relatives who had come to see them off. No matter how loudly they shouted and sang their farewells, the cacophony of ships' horns drowned them out. For Reinhard and Anni, however, there was nobody to see them off; their tearful farewell had already taken place in Germany some days before. Tears flowed as the coastline of Italy slipped away, but there was never a thought of turning back — they were Africa-bound at last. Reinhard hugged his wife and child. Although Kai-Uwe was only six months old, Anni was pregnant again. Their next baby would be born in Africa.

They were leaving Germany on a high note, and many supporters would be praying for them. But Reinhard and Anni were under no illusions. The wind of change was blowing over Africa, large parts of the continent were in turmoil, and conditions in South Africa were increasingly unsettled over the government's racist apartheid policy. It was not going to be easy and Reinhard had a feeling that he may also have problems with the mission board, but nothing could detract from the excitement he felt in his spirit — God had called him to Africa, and that was all that mattered.

The Middle East, too, was in a frenzy even as they sailed and there was some concern on board. The ship's bulletins were watched anxiously as Egypt and Israel moved towards war. It was a great relief when they passed safely through the Suez Canal. Soon afterwards, they ran into rough weather and Anni fell ill, and being in the early days of a pregnancy she needed medical attention. They were very glad when at the end of May 1967, they disembarked at Durban.

As they stepped ashore they were warmly welcomed by a delegation from the Apostolic Faith Mission (AFM), one of the oldest Pentecostal Fellowships in South Africa, with whom the German BFP were in co-operative fellowship and under whom Reinhard would be working for one year of probation.

Their first home was at Ermelo, in the Transvaal, where Anni gave birth to their second child, a daughter, Gabriele Felicitas. Anni loved Africa from the start. She was a tremendous help and example during this time. She was always unflinchingly at his side, not only finding time to be wife and mother but missionary as well.

The year soon turned out to be the toughest and most frustrating of Reinhard's life. He was required to submit to the standard missionary constitution which meant he had to study under a local pastor to learn about the country and customs before being sent out. The restrictions placed upon him were trivial. He was not even allowed to preach and the AFM also wanted him to be ordained again as one of their ministers.

But even this was nothing compared with finding himself confronted with the apartheid system at first hand. The minister under whom he was placed was Revd Stephanus Spies. He was a minister of high standing but he did his utmost to indoctrinate Reinhard with apartheid. Reinhard and Anni had heard about apartheid, but seeing it in operation shocked them deeply.

He told Reinhard, 'When you preach to the black people you do not call them brothers and sisters.'

Reinhard could not believe his ears. 'Then what am I supposed to call them?' he asked.

'Call them men and women,' Spies replied.

'Brother Spies, if this gospel does not make them and us brothers and sisters in Christ, I do not wish to preach this gospel any more,' was Reinhard's reply. He was further appalled when Revd Spies instructed him, 'Do not shake hands with the black people.'

Reinhard said, 'How can you win a soul then? What would have happened to us if Jesus had come into this world with that attitude?'

Reinhard found himself in almost ceaseless conflict with his 'tutor' who was constantly demanding an explanation for various things he had done. This so-called year of probation was one in which he died a thousand deaths. Reinhard was not a political person at all, but he could respect political systems. When it came to the gospel, however, he refused to compromise.

Eventually Reinhard was driven to the point where he knew that this could not continue. He approached Revd Spies and asked if they could discuss the situation with the AFM President. 'Otherwise,' he said, 'I might as well go to Zambia if this is to continue. At least there I would be able to preach.'

Reinhard went to Johannesburg to have a frank meeting with the President, Dr Möller, who was wise enough to perceive the true situation and he issued instructions that Reinhard was to be given full scope and allowed to preach. In spite of all differences Revd Spies and Reinhard became true friends.

When at last he fulfilled his year of probation, what a relief it was to be able to exercise his God-given ministry. He was to continue working with the AFM, while receiving his financial support from the BFP in Germany. As he prayerfully considered the future, his attention was turned to Lesotho which used to be the old British Protectorate of Basutoland. He was certain this was where the Lord was leading him, and events confirmed the rightness of this decision. He and his family therefore moved temporarily to Ladybrand in the Orange Free State just over the border, being unable to find housing in Lesotho itself.

Here they found themselves in an area with a large population of Africans, the people they loved. This was closer to their hearts and Reinhard started to hold evangelistic meetings. He was like a caged bird set free, spreading his wings at last. This was why he had come to Africa! Reinhard loved the black people and they responded.

Once he was allowed to preach it was not long before his outstanding ability in the pulpit was realised, resulting in a flow of invitations to minister in many of the white churches in South Africa. In fact the pastor of one of the biggest churches was about to retire and he invited Reinhard to take over. To many this would have been a tempting offer indeed.

He replied, 'Brother, if I wanted to preach to white people there are plenty back home in Germany. I did not come to Africa for the white people. I came for the black people. God sent me to the black people and I want to go where nobody else wants to go.'

As he was still working with the AFM he asked and received their permission to establish a new work in Maseru, the capital of this mountainous kingdom. It was a landlocked country with most of its people extremely poor, struggling to scrape a living from the land as there was hardly any industrialisation. Thousands of the young Basuto men left home each year to work in the gold mines of South Africa, but separated from their families it was a soul-destroying existence for which no amount of extra hard-earned money could compensate. When he first visited the place Reinhard sensed a depressing spirit of helplessness and hopelessness. With the sadness of Maseru still upon him, he sought guidance and received it clearly from God's word. He knew that this was where he had to start his work for God in Africa.

In 1969 the Bonnke family rejoiced in another happy event, the birth of their third child, another daughter, Susanne Herta, and it was in May of that same year that at last they were able to rent a simple two bedroomed house in Maseru. Living among the black people was marvellous. Reinhard said, 'We wanted to totally identify with them and it was wonderful living among the people we loved.' He always stressed that they came from Germany and did not believe in apartheid, which gave them acceptance. They quickly settled in, and as always, Reinhard set about planting fruit trees in the garden. They now had three children, a small house with intermittent supplies of electricity and running water, yet Anni loved every minute of it!

On many weekends the family would set off on Friday in their VW camping van to hold meetings in the mountains. Reinhard would preach, usually in English, with an interpreter, and then they would return on Sunday. They discovered that 'Bonnke' means 'everyone together' in Zulu, so often the people were expecting a black preacher! Reinhard would take every opportunity to preach the gospel — he even accepted to 'officiate' at many funerals seeing them as wonderful opportunities to 'throw out the net'. He was among the people to whom God had sent him, and he was happy.

But there were many weekends when Anni was left alone with the children. Later on two other missionary couples joined them, and they were able to work a 'rota' system of child minding. When she could she led women's meetings, teaching practical skills like knitting as well as the word of God, and on occasion travelled herself with the other missionary wives to remote villages. On one occasion they got a puncture, and were caught in a torrential rain storm. In such conditions it was not unknown for vehicles to be washed away, and for once the men were the ones at home praying for their safe return.

Before they had come to Africa, Anni had attended the Swansea Bible College for three months in order to learn English, though she could still speak only a few words. However, while she was there she came into contact with the missionaries' children who had been 'left behind' by their parents. Anni had seen how some of them had suffered, feeling rejected and unwanted, and was determined to try to avoid having to do the same with her own.

So in the course of time, when Kai-Uwe was old enough to go to school, he attended locally, and was for some time the only white child. Even so, their German origins brought their own difficulties. One day little Kai-Uwe returned home in tears, saying, 'Papa, they tease me about my name.'

Reinhard considered his second name, Friedrich, as an alternative, but that too was very German. 'I know,' he said to his son, 'we'll call you "Freddy" for short,' a name which stuck. At the same time, the Bonnke family took the decision to use English in the home to make it easier for the children who were swamped with so many languages. Nevertheless, Freddy very quickly picked up the local Sesotho, and much to Anni's surprise also learned Afrikaans. Often he would act as interpreter for her when someone came to the door who could not speak any English.

Following the pattern of her childhood, Anni kept an open house. In fact, on their second wedding anniversary, Reinhard had commented that it was only the second time in their life together that there had just been two of them at the dining table! More often than not, there were guests at the table. Black and white were all treated the same. Reinhard had witnessed and abhorred the system that segregated people based upon race and was determined that his family would make no such distinctions.

The nineteen years in which he was based in South Africa gave Reinhard an insight into the evils of apartheid. Now that at long last it has been abolished, everyone is ashamed of it, but what grieved Reinhard was that some of the hardest views in favour of apartheid were to be found inside the church. So many white preachers said they were against apartheid but in the cold light of reality all too many of them acquiesced. The cry to visiting European preachers was usually, 'You don't understand ... if you lived here you would think differently.' But Reinhard lived there for nineteen years and still could not understand!

Once in their new home, Reinhard's energies were able to be expressed without restriction. He was now free to preach and play his musical instruments and it was not very long before the city of Maseru was aware of his presence. He started holding open-air gospel services in the city bus station. By means of an interpreter and his accordion he was soon communicating the good news of salvation to the groups whose curiosity was aroused at the unusual sight of a tall, blond, white man making such happy music and speaking with such enthusiasm about Jesus Christ.

He found the bus station strategic, some days holding as many as four open-air meetings there. As a true evangelist he revelled in the opportunity of reaching the unbelievers, and did not hesitate right there in that busy place to make an appeal for people to receive Christ. The Holy Spirit began to work on the hearts and minds of these warm-hearted, unsophisticated people and they responded.

Among several to respond at these early meetings was Michael Kolisang. A young man of twenty-one he was interested in making a future in politics, but the message of the gospel gripped him and he accepted Christ. He could not speak any English and so it was through his interpreter that Reinhard had the joy of leading him to Christ, seated in his car. He was a true convert and from that moment he stuck with Reinhard and became one of his key workers. It was not very long before he was baptised with the Holy Spirit and under Reinhard's guidance and teaching he made rapid progress. Michael had not been privileged with a good education, but now he had an incentive as he wanted to study the Bible and equip himself to serve Christ in his needy country.

Reinhard's evangelism and passion for souls is infectious. From early in his ministry he realised the importance of making soul-winners as well as winning souls and in Michael he found a keen student. Michael quickly developed into a great soul-winner, and God gave him a ministry of healing which is so important in a country like Lesotho. Over many years he has laboured with Reinhard in many of his campaigns, and today Michael Kolisang is one of the most outstanding men of God in that land. To this day God continues to prosper and bless him in the winning of souls and the planting of new churches — and it all began in a bus station.

Reinhard loved to gather the black people around him and many times after he had been leading groups of new converts to Christ, he found himself asking as he checked through the names, 'Was this one black or white?' He was so much at home among all these people that colour did not register with him. Character and a person's heart were the essentials of life.

Now working as a district missionary of the AFM, he established a new church in Maseru and by dint of hard work the congregation grew to fifty. The church office was next door to the office of the Lesotho Communist Party, with just a thin wall between them. Reinhard said, 'We heard them cursing, and they heard us praying.' One afternoon a group of these Communists met Reinhard outside the office, and began to blaspheme the name of Jesus. Suddenly he felt the Holy Spirit filling his heart and he burst out, 'In the name of the one whom you are cursing now, I tell you that within less than a year your feet will no more walk upon these streets.' Immediately, he knew that the words were prophetic. What no one had foreseen was that a few months later Prime Minister Leabua Jonathan declared a state of emergency, and all Communists were rounded up and put into jail.

A similar incident occurred with a woman who went around telling evil lies about the church. Reinhard prayed that somehow the Lord would stop her, and soon afterwards, returning from a campaign, he heard that she had been struck dumb. Both Reinhard and the local people were shaken by these things.

Although he was constantly preaching the gospel in the surrounding townships and villages, it was still not enough for Reinhard and next he designed and wrote a Bible correspondence course. In five basic lessons, he had it translated into Sesotho and later into other languages. It was an immediate success and thousands were soon enrolled. He recruited people to mark the papers and those who completed the course received a certificate with a red seal upon it.

Its success led to the purchase of a small offset printing press from a friend in the Orange Free State. The course continued to prosper and soon a bigger press was needed to cope with the printing involved. Before long he was asking his friends in Germany to send him a printer to handle the press, and a volunteer was dispatched. All of this ultimately resulted in the purchase of a big press which was put up in the garage. At its peak some 50,000 people were taking the course. Having got his printer from Germany he was soon making full use of it. He started producing a high quality, evangelistic magazine called the *Apostolic Message*.

It has been a common feature of many outstanding evangelists that they could have been very successful businessmen. Reinhard, like many Germans, is a born organiser, being both thorough and enterprising but always with one object in view — reaching the lost for Christ. His next inspiration was bicycle evangelism. Many of the men in his church were unemployed with no prospect of a job and he saw how he could help them at the same time as harnessing their potential to spread the gospel.

He gathered them together and told them of his venture. Those who were willing would have the use of a bicycle which would be fitted with a strong, lockable box. They would be sent around the whole region systematically from house to house, handing out the magazine free and selling low cost hymn books and Bibles, for Reinhard had discovered that one of the hymn books was a ready seller and he would train those who were out of work to be both soul-winners and salesmen — and pay commission on all their sales.

They jumped at the opportunity. At first there were five of them, then ten, then as many as thirty. He found people to give money to purchase the bicycles and off went this little army of mobile colporteurs for Christ. They were backed up by prayer and they returned with joy to share wonderful stories of selling books and winning souls. They were soon earning twice the normal wage. As a result of that experience some of them became soul-winners and ultimately pastors.

The African ministry of Reinhard Bonnke was beginning to take shape, but more opposition awaited him. Not everyone was happy with his success. One above all saw the danger to his kingdom of darkness, and soon Reinhard's life was in danger.

Chapter 10

In Deadly Earnest

It was a searing hot afternoon in Lesotho and with the sun blazing down it felt like a blast furnace in the car. Stopping for a brief break in the village of Kolonyama, the cup of water looked so cool and inviting to Reinhard after hours of driving over the dusty mountain roads around Maseru visiting some of his pastors. The water looked clean and his throat was as dry as a desert so he took it gratefully and gulped it down. He should have known better as he had been in Africa long enough now to understand that drinking unboiled water was always risky. It was a moment of carelessness he was to regret.

He got safely home to Maseru that evening without any problem but during the night he became extremely ill. At first they thought it was a bout of dysentery but by morning he was worse and becoming delirious with a raging fever. Anni prayed desperately and did everything she could to bring the fever down. She also sent an urgent message to the believers, 'The Moruti [pastor] is sick, please pray for him.' As soon as they heard, some of the local pastors came and prayed for him but the second day passed without any improvement in his condition — the very opposite in fact. The fever was unabated and Reinhard was growing weaker and losing consciousness.

By the third day Anni's every instinct told her that it was an extremely serious situation for her, thousands of miles from home, with two young children and a baby, and a husband at death's door. She knew only too well that Africa was dotted with the graves of missionaries who had perished with black water fever and other deadly fevers in the last two centuries.

As he slipped in and out of consciousness Reinhard, too, sensed the danger he was in. During one moment as he lay there with his eyes open, feeling helpless and weak, he saw what seemed like a black blanket descending upon him as though to envelop him in its suffocating folds of darkness. An instinctive foreboding warned him that death was seeking to claim him. He summoned his spiritual strength to resist but physically he was so drained that resistance seemed beyond him.

At that moment, thousands of miles away in Germany it was morning and a devoted woman member of his father's church had got up early to pray. As she gave herself to prayer she felt a special burden to pray for Reinhard. Immediately she felt the anointing of the Holy Spirit as she began to intercede and she became aware that his life was somehow in danger. A woman of intercession, Frau Eliese Köhler knew that this was no ordinary situation, and she cried to God, pleading, agonising, wrestling in prayer until the burden lifted. She spent virtually the whole of that day in prayer until she believed that her prayers had prevailed, but she had no earthly way of knowing — only the sweet assurance of the Holy Spirit and the peace of God.

Back in Africa, a weakened Reinhard stared upwards as the blanket of blackness continued its dark descent ... then suddenly its black opaqueness was less intense and through it he was sure he could see the face of Jesus. A sense of peace and comfort came over him and he was conscious that someone was praying. He heard a voice crying out to God, pleading in prayer for his life. He had heard it many times in the prayer meetings in his father's church, and he recognised it as that of Eliese Köhler. The blanket of blackness faded and he drifted peacefully into a restful sleep; the fever had broken and the crisis was over.

It still took him several weeks to recover his health but as soon as he was fit he wrote a letter home to Hermann and told him about the whole incident. He gave the date and time and asked him to get in touch with Frau Köhler to find out what had happened to her on that day. She confirmed that it was the same day and time that she had prayed for him. It was a tremendous encouragement to her, and a witness to Hermann and his church of the amazing power of prayer and the awesome responsibility of being an intercessor. To Reinhard and Anni it was another demonstration of the importance of prayer support when engaged in the battle for souls.

Although the correspondence course was proving very popular, Reinhard saw that the potential of some of the new believers warranted personal training. He discussed the matter with the AFM leaders but eventually the concept was dropped when it was opposed by the South African government who made it all too clear that they did not want him sending lots of black students down to the Bible Colleges in South Africa. The only solution was to start one of his own in Maseru. The AFM readily granted him permission to do this under their auspices and before long he began a Bible School with five students.

He recruited Michael Kolisang to help him. Reinhard became the Principal and Anni, always willing to help whatever demands seemed to be made upon her, did the cooking. In common with everything else Reinhard touched, the Bible School prospered and soon there were twenty students, and eventually forty. Before long they engaged a full-time cook, and a well-educated white woman to teach English, and help with the equivalent of O-levels. Reinhard taught evangelism and biblical theology.

It must be said that the AFM were generous in their support and sent the fledgling Bible School study materials and other basic necessities. They also officially recognised the school which was a help in dealing with the authorities. The school had every privilege and Reinhard's thoroughness ensured that it was well organised. The students were sent out preaching at the weekends and gained valuable practical experience in evangelism.

All of these activities: the colporteurs on their bicycles (and one or two on horseback for some of the mountainous areas); the printing press and the new gospel magazine; the Bible correspondence course; the Bible School; the new church; all dovetailed together to form a constant programme of aggressive evangelism and training. It was a seedbed for the future and provided Reinhard with invaluable experience. It worked like clockwork. The colporteurs returned every few weeks to replenish their stocks of literature, pay in their takings and receive their commission. Many people were won for Christ and in two years virtually the whole country of Lesotho was covered.

The only thing missing at this stage was a tent — and one was forthcoming. It was old and well used but it was a gift to Reinhard and served to get him started with a gospel tent in Lesotho. Unfortunately the canvas was so sun-bleached and weathered that the first storm ripped it to pieces. However, it had proved its worth and Reinhard's appetite for tent evangelism in Africa had been whetted. One weekend when he was away preaching in an AFM church at Pietermaritsburg they were so stirred by the reports of what was happening in Lesotho that they gave him money for a brand new tent and a generator as well. The new tent was soon in full use. They pitched it wherever they could, and it was used not only by Reinhard and his teams of students but by some Basuto evangelists as well.

He was still serving his apprenticeship as a missionary. His salary in 1970 was 110 rands per month — a pittance, but in line with that of missionaries of the majority of Western mission boards at the time. It was impossible to do all that he was without extra support for these many projects, but this was readily forthcoming from supporters and friends in Germany as well as generous churches like the one at Pietermaritsburg. He kept a careful account of all such money and these figures were always open for inspection. Indeed, his associates sometimes felt that his scrupulous integrity was pernickety — if it was a personal item he always insisted on paying for it out of his own pocket, right down to a postage stamp.

Then one night Reinhard had a dream that would change his life for ever. He saw a map of Africa, and as he watched he saw it being washed in red blood. The Holy Spirit told him it was the blood of Jesus, and whispered into his ear, 'Africa shall be saved!' When he awoke from the dream he was both alarmed and thrilled. The next night the same dream came to him, and was repeated over many nights. He began to ask the Lord, 'Why are you showing this to me? I am stuck here in Lesotho preaching to a few people at a time. How can the whole continent be saved this way?' He calculated that it would take thousands of years. Nevertheless, the vision grew in his heart, until he began to preach, 'Africa shall be saved! Africa shall be saved!'

His ever-expanding vision began to make a few officials nervous both in Germany and in South Africa. As early as 1972 he was talking about a gospel enterprise to take the message of Christ from Cape Town to Cairo. That kind of talk is guaranteed to give the average member of most church boards sleepless nights. It was true that he was not asking them for money for these daring ventures but some were understandably afraid that they may be left to foot the bill if anything went wrong. In very many things the AFM did not restrict him. Although he still submitted to the District Council of the Orange Free State to whom he was immediately answerable, he was free to follow his vision in Lesotho. They were kind and supported him, inviting him to their churches — so much so that he had to be careful to see that his priority was not preaching in white churches but to the black people who needed him most.

The break when it came did not come with the AFM but with the German Missions Board, and it did not come immediately. Though there were tensions Reinhard was anxious to remain within the two Fellowships both at home in Germany, and on the field in South Africa. He is not an isolationist, for he appreciates the whole body of Christ. However, the irritations continued.

The new magazine was a great success and a vital arm of the colporteur work, but one official was not happy that Reinhard had chosen to name his printing press the AFM Press. 'Then what shall I call it?' he asked 'Every child needs a name, and this new printing press needs a name too.'

'Call it anything,' said the official, 'anything, that is, except our title "Apostolic"!'

Reinhard submitted and that was almost certainly the first time that 'Christ for all Nations' was used, a title dropped into his heart by the Holy Spirit.

By this time the Bible correspondence course had been going for five years and having reached the amazing enrolment of 50,000, its very success was proving to be costly. Reinhard was constantly having to scratch around to find money to keep it going. The cost of envelopes and postage alone for such a venture was considerable. To achieve 'more with less' he even bought envelopes in bulk, 100,000 at a time, but that meant saving up a considerable amount of cash before he could order them.

Driving one day to Bloemfontein, he was engaged in a prayerful conversation with the Lord over finance. He had recently had an unpleasant experience involving a financial deal and he was still questioning the Lord over what had happened.

It was his heart for the poor pastors which had led him into the unfortunate affair. In the same building where he rented two offices for the correspondence course and other outreach work, there was a catalogue business dealing in furniture at bargain prices. He knew the extreme poverty of his black pastors and was moved when he saw how little furniture they had in their humble homes. The pastors had seen the catalogues when they made their routine calls to the offices, and could not believe the low prices. For the first time in their lives they saw things even they could afford, with a little help!

They asked Reinhard if he would assist them with the finance and he could not resist their persuasive pleas. As always he brought the matter prayerfully before the Lord and he felt that their poverty and devotion to their calling warranted him helping them. He decided that he was going to do something he had never done before in his life. He was going to borrow money and lend it to these pastors. The pastors and their wives were overjoyed at his willingness to help, and ordered their furniture — tables, chairs, and other basic things. They would repay him as they were able.

The price was so cheap that Reinhard asked the salesman how he could sell furniture at such rock bottom prices. Like all salesmen he gave Reinhard a plausible assurance that everything was above board; he had nothing to worry about. So Reinhard signed the order and paid the money in advance and waited. It would be twenty-eight days before delivery.

A month later he received a frantic phone call from one of the pastors. It transpired that the deal was illegal because the furniture was being imported from South Africa and government restrictions did not allow this in Lesotho on goods bought on hire purchase agreements. The pastor had also learned that the salesman was about to disappear over the border leaving them with nothing but a big debt and possible trouble with the authorities. He finished the phone call pleading with Reinhard to get a lawyer immediately to see what could be done.

Reinhard's heart sank as he tried to take in all the implications, and he wondered which lawyer to contact. Prayer comes naturally in such circumstances but often it *is* natural and devoid of faith. But Reinhard bowed his head and said, 'Lord Jesus, you are my lawyer; I put this case in your hands.' Naive? The pastor almost certainly thought so next morning when he called on him and asked if he had been able to get hold of a lawyer.

'Yes, the best in town.'

'And who is that?' asked the pastor. His relief evaporated into a cloud of quizzical uncertainty when Reinhard calmly replied with that boyish smile of his, 'Jesus! I'm resting my case with Jesus.'

The events which immediately followed could not have done much to allay the pastor's doubts. The salesman fled the country, the pastors did not get their furniture, and Reinhard was left with the debt. He told no one about the incident, feeling ashamed that he had allowed himself to be taken in. But at the same time the Lord knew his heart and that it was not for himself but for others who were in genuine need.

A few days later he was preaching at a church some distance away and as he was leaving a man pressed an envelope into his hand, saying, 'This is a gift for your personal use.' When he had opportunity to open it he found to his joyous astonishment that it was double the amount that he owed on the furniture deal. He paid it off with great relief and was able to tell the pastor and his friends that the affair was now closed, and he added, 'And my lawyer does not charge any fees — isn't that wonderful?'

Perhaps the doubting pastor remembered the words of the Lord Jesus, who said, 'I praise you, Father, Lord of heaven and earth, because you have hidden these things from the wise and learned, and revealed them to little children. Yes, Father, for this was your good pleasure' (Luke 10:21). God was teaching his servant the priceless value of such a childlike spirit.

Reinhard was still mulling over the incident as he drove to Bloemfontein, praying about the constant pressure of raising finance for the correspondence course, especially the bulk order of envelopes. Suddenly the glory of God seemed to fill the car and Reinhard found himself weeping, feeling as though he was in heaven. He had no words to describe it.

'I was no longer conscious of driving the car. I felt as though I was being wrapped up in God's glory and posted to heaven.'

All thoughts of the furniture mishap and the bill for 100,000 envelopes vanished and he heard a voice say, 'The flour in the barrel shall not diminish and the oil in the cruse shall not become less.'

With the same suddenness with which it had come, the glory lifted and he was still driving serenely and safely along the highway, but the words of the promise were vibrating with power in his heart. He was familiar with the incident of Elijah and the widow woman in 1 Kings 17:14, and he knew in his spirit that God was giving him a promise as sure as that which he had given to the widow through Elijah long ago. Reinhard had two mission accounts at the bank, and he believed that God was assuring him that his cry was heard and that as long as he was faithful in pouring out the 'flour' and the 'oil' from the accounts God would be responsible for seeing that they were constantly replenished. He believed God and embraced the promise, and from that moment he knew that he had entered into a different realm of faith and finance for the kingdom of God.

He testifies: 'After that experience, I have never managed to get into the red with the work that God sent me to do in Africa. I have sometimes overspent only to find that the amount was met by some anonymous deposit.' God knew that he had arrived at a place where he could be trusted not to abuse such a promise. Those near to him, especially his treasurers, will confirm that while many times he has nearly caused them heart failure as he has outlined some great new venture of faith for the kingdom of God, it is never for himself, and the money has always come.

God was preparing him for greater things but God never hurries his preparation and never cuts corners. It is generally agreed that Elisha served a ten-year-long apprenticeship as Elijah's servant before he was entrusted with his mantle. Reinhard had a few more trials and disappointments to face before his apprenticeship was finished.

Chapter 11

Plundering Hell to Populate Heaven

During his years in Lesotho, Reinhard sometimes found himself preaching to just five people, and despite all his efforts, there were times when if he had an audience of fifty at one of his meetings in Maseru it was almost like revival. Seasoned workers tried to reassure him with the platitude, 'Everybody knows Lesotho is a hard place and really you are doing well.' But he could never accept this philosophy. The burden of Africa's 450 million people weighed heavily upon him. His various outreaches revealed that there was a fantastic harvest out there, ripe and ready to be reaped by anyone bold enough to believe God for bigger and better things. Five years' experience in Africa only confirmed his conviction that the key to world evangelisation was aggressive preaching of the gospel of Christ in the power of the Holy Spirit with accompanying signs of miracles, healings and deliverances.

In 1973 it seemed to Reinhard that there was one man who would arouse Maseru if only he could be persuaded to come. This evangelist was stirring the nation of South Africa, making the headlines in the daily papers with stories of healings and of great crowds. It was all the more dramatic because he was from the Dutch Reform Church, but through the world wide wave of Holy Spirit renewal which was affecting many of the historic churches, he had been greatly blessed and his ministry had become charismatic.

So desperate was Reinhard to get him to come to Maseru that he went to the evangelist's home in Pretoria to deliver the invitation in person. To his joy, the great evangelist agreed to come to Lesotho for two services over one weekend, Saturday evening and Sunday morning. When Reinhard returned, his news that the evangelist was going to come to Maseru was greeted with terrific enthusiasm. The preparations were put in hand and everything possible was done to ensure that the visit received maximum publicity. Their printing press rolled off thousands and thousands of handbills and posters. With such a well-known name they even managed to get time on the local radio station.

Expectations were running high when the weekend finally arrived. Above all they had prayed and Reinhard was confident that this could produce the breakthrough he had been longing for ever since he had set foot in Maseru. It needed a great demonstration of God's power in healing and deliverance to break the hold of generations of witchcraft, superstition and occult practices.

On the Saturday evening the church building was packed, and among those present were many sick and needy people, including the lame and blind. As Reinhard gazed down from the platform upon this great crowd his heart cried out to God for him to move in power. The situation was everything he had envisaged and when the evangelist rose to preach he had their attention and kept it. But then quite unexpectedly he turned to Reinhard and urged him to close the service.

'But the people are expecting you to pray for the sick,' replied Reinhard, but the evangelist was adamant. He wanted the meeting ended.

Reinhard was embarrassed and concerned. 'I will then, but you must promise to pray for them in the morning.' Hastily it was agreed and the service ended abruptly. The crowds dispersed, the church was locked, and he wondered how many would return.

Reinhard rose early, and to his surprise he found even more people at the church than on the previous evening. Assured all was well, he went to collect the evangelist. He arrived just as the great man was loading his suitcase into a waiting car. Perplexed and anxious, Reinhard asked him, 'What is happening?'

His reply staggered him: 'I'm going home.'

'Going home?' spluttered Reinhard. 'You mustn't ... you can't do that. The church is already packed ... they are expecting you, and others are still arriving.'

The evangelist looked at him and declared in a way that left no room for argument, 'The Holy Spirit told me I must go.'

The statement knocked all the wind out of Reinhard. What could he say to that? He knew that he had to accept it. He was left alone to face the music! There was only one thing he could do at that moment — pray!

'O God,' he cried, 'I am not a big name preacher, I am a missionary, one of your little men, but Lord I will preach today and I believe that you will work the miracles. In your name I will stop playing marbles, and start moving mountains!'

The first mountain he had to move was the dejection of the local pastors when he told them that the evangelist had gone. Neither did they show a great deal of enthusiasm when he told them, 'I am going to preach and God will do miracles.' He said it with a confidence that shook even himself and the pastors rallied behind him. The next mountain was the great crowd of folk waiting in the packed church. Without beating about the bush he told them what had happened and that he, Mr Bonnke from Germany, their regular missionary, would be preaching and praying for the sick. A couple got up and left, but their seats near the front were quickly filled by others from the back.

As soon as Reinhard stood to preach, the atmosphere which had seemed so dull the previous evening was charged with the presence of God. Reinhard was conscious of a tremendous anointing of the Holy Spirit, and even as he preached, new insight came to him as he expounded the word of God. It was alive, his faith was rising and so was that of the congregation. He was ministering faith, and he was revealing Jesus as he opened the Scriptures. Suddenly, halfway through the sermon, the interpreter fell to the ground under the power of the Spirit. The crowd were so taken up with what Jesus was doing they forgot the missing evangelist.

As Reinhard waited for his interpreter to recover, God spoke to him, the words acting like fire upon his faith: 'My word in *your* mouth is as strong as my word in *my* mouth.'

The interpreter scrambled to his feet with a little help from Reinhard who could hardly wait to continue preaching, the message burning in his heart. He had never experienced anything to match this in all his ministry. Then the Holy Spirit spoke a second time: 'Call those who are totally blind and speak the word of authority.' It was an awesome moment, and he trembled to obey. With a catch in his voice he asked, 'Will all the totally blind people please stand up?' Half a dozen sightless figures stood to their feet, their ears straining to take in every precious word from the pulpit. As he looked at the daunting need, unwelcome doubts suddenly invaded his mind: 'What if nothing happens?' He knew the source of such thoughts and resisted the devil with all his determination. 'I am going to do what Jesus told me to do.'

Boldly he declared, 'I am going to speak with the authority God has given me and you are going to see a white man standing in front of you. Your eyes are going to be opened.'

It was a challenge — especially now that the big preacher had left. Many respected Reinhard Bonnke, but they knew that if nothing happened every witch-doctor for miles around would crow with delight and the cause of Christ in Maseru would receive a definite setback.

Reinhard drew a deep breath and shouted, 'In the name of Jesus, blind eyes open!' Suddenly one of the sightless ones, a woman, screamed out with an ear-piercing shriek, 'I can see, I can see, I can see!'

This woman who, it was learned afterwards, had been blind for four years, rushed towards Reinhard, grabbing people as she went, demonstrating to them that she could see again. When the congregation realised what had happened, they erupted into a bedlam of excited shouts of praise and rejoicing. When order was restored, the woman stood at the rostrum beside him and proved that she could now see well enough to read, and the rejoicing burst out afresh.

In that atmosphere it seemed that anything could happen and it did. A young mother with a crippled child in her arms passed him over the heads of the solid crowd to Reinhard. The very passing of this little bundle of childhood released a wave of love and faith with every touch. Reinhard was no longer on his own — every believer there was transformed into a minister, and everyone was expecting more miracles.

Reinhard took the helpless child in his arms, prayed in the name of Jesus, and felt a flow of God's power go through the little body. As he watched he saw the tiny legs moving and pulsating with life. He was staggered with joy at what he was seeing and in faith he put the tiny crippled boy down on the floor. He stood for a second or two and then took a step and as his legs straightened before their eyes he began to run all over the platform. There was no stopping the meeting then. Every fresh healing was greeted with new shouts of joy, and now all the black pastors shared the ministry too. The healings and conversions and singing and rejoicing went on for most of the day.

Maseru would never be the same again. It was a day when the Lord had visited his people in power. Reinhard knew as he lingered alone in the church after the crowds had finally gone home that he could never be the same again either. Elated and exhausted, blessed but humbled, he lifted his heart to God and gave God all the glory and pledged himself to pursue this new ministry which God had given him to the uttermost. That day he had experienced something more of the powers of the world to come, and knew at last that this was the way to reach the continent of Africa for Christ.

He was still somewhat bewildered at the way it had happened. When the evangelist said, 'The Holy Spirit told me to go,' Reinhard accepted that it was the only explanation — it had to be God's doing. God was teaching two men lessons that day, one who was humble enough to leave when God told him to; the other bold enough to grasp an opportunity when it was presented to him.

This divinely engineered breakthrough in 1973 greatly boosted Reinhard's expanding vision. One day soon afterwards, Reinhard said to his wife, 'Anni, I asked the Lord today for thirty dollars for the rent for the offices, and what do you think? He asked me if I would like a million dollars.'

Anni looked at him and said, 'That sounds wonderful ... and you thanked him and said, "Yes please, Lord"?'

'No I didn't ... I was going to when I thought of how much good I could do with a million dollars. But then I knew in my heart I could ask for something much better, and I said, "No, Lord, don't give me a million dollars. Rather Lord, give me a million souls for Christ."'

Anni was thrilled. This passion for the lost was why she loved him, and she had a feeling that his response had pleased the Lord too. She was even more sure when he told her, 'And you know what? I was sure the Lord whispered into my heart that we would plunder hell and populate heaven ... I thought they were some of the most wonderful words I have ever heard.'

The expanding vision thrilled some, but the German Mission Board were increasingly anxious about the financial implications of these growing ventures. A long correspondence culminated in a visit to Maseru by the Director of the German Missions Board, Revd Gottfried Starr. Reinhard was hopeful that the chance to talk things over personally would help them to resolve matters.

Unfortunately the visit proved to be difficult for all concerned. The Director was delighted when he was shown the printing press, the Bible School, the correspondence course offices, the church, and the tent, but he made it clear that the Board was not happy with all these extra activities. Although Reinhard accepted full responsibility for raising the necessary funds, if a debt situation ever arose, he said that they would be the ones who were liable. 'Therefore,' said the Director, 'we cannot allow you to expand.'

When he left to return to Germany, Reinhard wondered what he should do. This proposed curtailment of his extra activities was like a death knell to his burning soul. After discussing it with Anni they agreed to wait until he received the official notification of the decision. Several weeks later they confirmed starkly, 'You may not expand.'

He stared at it, desolate. 'Anni, I have to go to some secluded place where I can sort this out before the Lord. I will not return until I know that I have heard from God.' She hugged him, assured him of her love and support and watched him leave.

Alone with God, Reinhard poured out his soul and made no attempt to hide his feelings from the Lord: 'O God, I am sick and tired of all this fighting and hassle. Lord, let me agree with my brethren and let me live in peace with them.'

Heaven's reply was prompt and plain: 'If you drop my call I will have to look for somebody else — and I will have to drop you.'

He knew that God had spoken and his response was equally prompt and definite. He jumped up from his knees and went home to his waiting and anxious wife.

'Anni,' he declared, 'I am resigning today from the German Mission.'

He told her what God had said to him and without more ado and with her full support he sat down and wrote out the letter of resignation. He had no peace until the letter was posted — the moment that was done the peace of God filled his soul.

His next task was to phone Dr F.P. Möller, President of the AFM Board. He told him that he had resigned from the German Mission and therefore he must also say goodbye to the AFM as well. Dr Möller had become a good friend to Reinhard and held him in high regard and he was very upset at the news. 'You have done what? You have resigned and you did not speak to me first?' Dr Möller begged him, 'Please withdraw your letter of resignation at least to give me a chance to talk to our friends in Germany.' Dr Möller went so far as to say that the AFM would pay the expenses to bring out to South Africa the German leader, Reinhold Ulonska, to discuss the whole matter.

Reinhard agreed, and wrote a second letter withdrawing his resignation in the hope that an acceptable solution could be found. He was anxious to do all in his power to maintain fellowship with all concerned. At short notice, Reinhold Ulonska flew out to South Africa and conferred with Dr Möller and with Reinhard. Dr Möller emphasised that the AFM did not want to lose Reinhard if that could be avoided. Revd Ulonska, however, made it clear that the German Board felt that they could not treat Reinhard any differently from their other missionaries.

'But he is different from the other missionaries,' replied Dr Möller. 'We wish we had many more like him.' And of course, that was the problem. The 'system' could not cope.

Ultimately they agreed to give Reinhard his freedom — to let him go. Reinhard said, 'I only want to leave with your blessing, if you will tell the German Fellowship that you have asked me to launch out on my own.'

They readily agreed, although the announcement of the fact that they had asked him to set up his own organisation ran into delays. However, it was the only acceptable solution. It was clear that Reinhard's many outreaches could not be curtailed.

It was painful for all concerned, and it says much for the grace and maturity of all that they bowed to the inevitable. Over the years there has been no acrimony between them and the bond between the AFM, the German Pentecostal Fellowship and Reinhard Bonnke continues to grow.

For Reinhard, severing the special links with his past was like leaving home all over again, only this time he was on a different continent, with a wife and three precious children to support. It proved to be even more painful than either he or Anni had anticipated.

Chapter 12

A Vision for Africa ...

The many friends they had made in Lesotho were sad at the thought of losing Reinhard, Anni and the children, but they all knew it was inevitable and thanked God that he had given them to Lesotho for those crucial years.

Dr Möller and the AFM did all they could to help in preparing for the change. During the closing months of 1974, as Reinhard prayed about the future, the one place that remained in his mind was the vision of Johannesburg. While there on a visit to AFM headquarters in October, Anni saw a new house in a suburb of Boksburg, called Witfield. Reinhard had felt the Holy Spirit say that his new base should be near Johannesburg international airport, and this was within easy driving distance.

So on the 6th December 1974 they finally left Lesotho for Witfield. The children were excited, Anni was busily planning in her mind the details of their new home, but Reinhard was just not his usual energetic self. At their new home when the furniture arrived, all Reinhard did was to sit on the suitcases. Anni was worried now; Reinhard seemed physically and spiritually drained.

With his head in his hands he sat there and prayed, 'Lord, I feel so hopeless. You spoke to me two years ago those thrilling words, "Africa shall be saved!" over and over again, night after night, until the vision of an Africa cleansed from its sin and sadness and suffering, blazed in my heart and I believed it would happen. But Lord, here I sit on our suitcases, ready to win the world for you, but I don't know how.'

Anni hoped that a good night's sleep would improve matters but there was no improvement. For four weeks it seemed to Reinhard as if God did not speak to him at all. For a man for whom communion with his Lord was the very breath of life, it was a deeply trying experience. In the end he was experiencing such pain in his stomach that he went to see a medical doctor friend who pronounced, 'Reinhard, you have got stomach ulcers.'

He immediately responded, 'I don't know what ulcers are. I cannot believe it. I have never had problems with my stomach.'

'Well,' said his friend, 'that is what you have got.'

That very night God spoke to Reinhard clearly at last: 'Fly to Gaborone in Botswana.' In the morning he found that his stomach was healed. Before long he was on his way.

Botswana, a desolate landlocked neighbour of South Africa, was the kind of place that needed a word from God for anyone to consider going there. Not having enough money for a taxi, he walked into the city, and God met with him right there on the street and spoke into his heart, 'Turn to the right.' He obeyed and found himself outside Botswana's National Sports Stadium, and again the Lord spoke into his heart: 'You will preach my name there.' The four weeks of silence was over.

His initial thought had been to use Botswana's radio station. Now he knew God wanted him to hold a campaign, so he sought out a local minister, Pastor Scheffers, and told him the news. The pastor was thrilled until Reinhard asked him to book the National Sports Stadium.

'That holds 10,000,' he told Reinhard, 'and I only get forty people in my church on a Sunday morning; wouldn't it be better to book a hall?'

'Book the biggest hall in the city and also make arrangements for us to book the National Sports Stadium, and I will be in touch.'

That was in January 1975, and he returned to Witfield to gather a team for his first big campaign in Africa. Anni was delighted to see that Reinhard was fully recovered but was astonished when he outlined his plans. However, the name 'Christ for all Nations' was already appearing outside their new base and she had a warm glow in her spirit about that. She also had a feeling in her heart that there were going to be many lonely days ahead, left at home with the children. But she accepted it as her part in winning Africa for Christ.

The campaign was fixed for April, but the churches in Gaborone were not proving very enthusiastic. Nonetheless in faith, the biggest hall in the city seating 800 was booked for the opening days of the campaign and the stadium for the closing part.

One man Reinhard wanted on his team was Richard Ngidi, a gifted Zulu preacher with a proven healing ministry. However, Reinhard was anxious to maintain good relations with the AFM, and did not want to appear to be poaching workers. So he asked God to make it happen in his own way. At a youth conference soon afterwards, Richard Ngidi called Reinhard over to him and told him that he wanted to work with him! They served God together for the next two years.

Their faith was quickly tested. Pastor Scheffers had covered the city with posters, but when Reinhard and his team stepped onto the platform they found themselves with a hundred people in the 800-seat hall. Reinhard assured them all that God was going to fill the hall before the campaign was through. As he preached, the power of God invested his every word with life and light and when Richard Ngidi began praying for the sick, many were demonstrably healed. Soon the hundred were making enough noise for a thousand, but then suddenly people started falling to the floor. It puzzled Reinhard and people began to ask, 'What is happening?' He considered it carefully, but since the presence of God was palpable he replied, 'The Bible speaks about signs and wonders, and surely this is a sign of God's presence.'

The news of what was happening spread across the city. Sinners were finding Christ as Saviour, the sick were getting healed of all kinds of afflictions, and people were collapsing to the floor, apparently overwhelmed by the presence of Almighty God. By the end of the first week some 2,000 were wanting to get in. During that week Reinhard observed every manifestation with great care and tested everything by the Scriptures and by the fruits of these unusual occurrences, and he was persuaded that 'it was of God' and he was not going to fight it.

When they moved to the 10,000-seat stadium it was soon thronged. The reality of the conversions was demonstrated with 500 people sealing their decision to receive Christ by being publicly baptised in water. Reinhard was overwhelmed with joy, but God had one more key to give him before the campaign closed.

God spoke again into Reinhard's heart, 'Pray for the people to be baptised with the Holy Spirit and power.' Reinhard had never thought of doing such a thing in a campaign. It was so different from the way he had been brought up. He asked one of his African team members to explain how to receive this experience, but his message left Reinhard feeling frustrated, for he did not mention speaking in tongues. When he decided to explain this himself, the Holy Spirit checked him, and, puzzled, he obediently remained seated.

How glad he was that he did so. About 1,000 people had moved forward when the invitation was given to those wanting to be baptised with the Holy Spirit. Reinhard led them in a simple prayer and as soon as they raised their hands in supplication it was as though a tornado had swept over them. In a matter of seconds they were flattened to the ground and began speaking in tongues, many of them prophesying as well. Reinhard stared with awe. Now he understood. No one could possibly say that they were speaking in other tongues because he had suggested it to them. This was God's doing. It was the first time he had witnessed a mass receiving of the baptism of the Holy Spirit. His part in it had been minimal, as though he had been asked to stand aside and let Christ work unhindered.

Wiping the tears from his eyes he lifted his heart to heaven and prayed, 'Oh Lord, as you have promised, pour out your Spirit on all flesh, throughout every part of the world, for your glory. Amen.'

In this tremendous campaign, God was showing him the pattern for his future ministry. But he also revealed that quite a few of Reinhard's German characteristics, such as this wanting to understand things before he obeyed, were more of a hindrance than a help in this realm of the Spirit. He realised he needed to open himself fully to the Lord and let him strip from him everything which quenched the working of the Holy Spirit.

Chapter 13

… and a Message for the World

Gaborone was undoubtedly the launching pad for Reinhard's burgeoning ministry. Back in Witfield, however, he was soon aware that although he had taken a giant leap forward in the perspective of 'Africa shall be saved', it was still only a small step. Although he was thrilled at the welcome home from Anni and the children and the new Christ for all Nations staff, he recalled the words of warning from Jesus: 'Do not rejoice that the spirits submit to you, but rejoice that your names are written in heaven' (Luke 10:20).

Having now moved into a ministry of signs and wonders, opportunities were multiplying. But after that tornado of God's Spirit at Gaborone he was positively persuaded that the key to world evangelism was the mass outpouring of the Holy Spirit which will break the devil's hold. Despite that, his conviction remained that his God-given ministry was that of an evangelist. He says, 'In our ministry I do not speak of "healing campaigns" but "gospel campaigns"... evangelism is my calling.' The message of salvation through Christ and his cross, his blood and his resurrection, was burning at white heat in his heart. To him, physical healing was important, but the salvation of the soul was all-important. 'Jesus saves from sin. Then the power of God is always present to heal.'

While gathering the team for Gaborone, he had become burdened by the needs of the sprawling African township of Soweto, on the outskirts of Johannesburg. The poverty and overcrowding of most of these people appalled him. Crime and disillusionment were endemic.

He determined to raise a force of 100 colporteur evangelists on bicycles, to cover the whole of Soweto house to house with personal evangelism and literature. The cost would be considerable, but Anni backed his plans; this was why God had brought them to Africa.

Reinhard and Anni prayed over the venture, and immediately people began calling to ask if they needed a bicycle for the mission work. Soon they had enough money to buy fifteen bicycles and Reinhard was so impressed at how quickly this whole venture seemed to be progressing that he said to Anni, 'It seems as though God is hurrying this project along — it's almost as if he is pushing us to get on with it as quickly as possible.' Later they would understand why they were being pushed, but then only God knew what lay ahead for Soweto.

Soon afterwards, a man approached him and offered the money needed for the remaining eighty-five bicycles. Rejoicing, Reinhard went to the factory and signed the contract but the benefactor then changed his mind. 'I am sorry,' he told Reinhard, 'I have made a mistake. I cannot give you anything.' Despite this setback, Reinhard continued to trust God, and his faith was rewarded. The money flowed in.

The team planned the campaign with military precision. In the office a huge map of Soweto filled a wall and the movements of the 100-strong force of bicycle evangelists were kept under constant prayer surveillance. The massive outreach went on for eight long months. The bicycle evangelists led many to Christ, saw many healed, and left literature in thousands of homes. One evangelist led to Christ a young man who confessed that he was a murderer; no sooner had they finished praying than the police broke into the house and arrested the new believer. Throughout these eventful months rumblings of unrest against apartheid had been mounting through the nation. Then on 18th June 1976, not long after the last evangelist had fulfilled his mission, large-scale rioting broke out in Soweto, and many were killed. Only then did Reinhard fully appreciate God's urgency to reach the township. It was another lesson he took to heart. Again he asked himself, 'What if I had not obeyed?' God's timing is always perfect.

For some time now Reinhard had been looking for ground to expand his headquarters for the growing work of CfaN. Early in 1976 he found an old farmhouse surrounded by overgrown land near to his home, and recognising its potential made an offer, even though he had no money. Three months later he was able to sit down and write out a cheque for the full amount — God had provided once again.

Meanwhile, Reinhard was already building up a busy campaign trail, and among other meetings and rallies he held a very successful campaign in Cape Town in November 1976. Richard Ngidi prayed for the sick while Reinhard preached the gospel. Reinhard and Richard worked together well in a living demonstration to the nation of a Christianity that is bigger than racism. In the Cape Town campaign there were outstanding conversions and remarkable healings, including cripples rising from their wheelchairs, one of whom was caught on camera.

Things were rapidly gathering pace and 1976, as well as seeing the successful conclusion of the Soweto outreach, found Reinhard and the Christ for all Nations team campaigning in Brighton, Port Elizabeth; in Katutura, Windhoek, in Namibia; and Swaziland, where Reinhard was given the opportunity of preaching to the royal household.

At Brighton, in the 4,000-seater Centenary Hall, hundreds made restitution of stolen goods, and others openly surrendered weapons and fetishes linked with witchcraft. Almost 2,000 made decisions to accept Christ as their Saviour. In the Katutura township campaign, Michael Kolisang took over the role of praying for the sick when Richard Ngidi could only spend one week there. Michael was to remain with the team for eighteen years.

This memorable year closed with the big campaign in the former British protectorate of Swaziland. The small kingdom is a fertile, landlocked enclave between Mozambique and South Africa, with a population of around three-quarters of a million. The campaign was held in two places, in Manzini, the largest city, with a population of some 50,000; and Mbabane, the capital, with a population of about 40,000.

The various campaigns throughout 1975 and 1976 had made it apparent to Reinhard that they needed a bigger tent. On this occasion all they had was a small 800-seat tent. Most of the crowd stood outside. In the middle of the Mbabane campaign there was a cloudburst which in moments turned the field into a quagmire. The tent was pitched on a slight slope and Reinhard watched, horrified but helpless, as torrents of water poured down the slope and through the tent. The sick and crippled were caught in the middle of the flood as they struggled to get onto the higher ground, but for most of them the effort was too much and all they could do was lie there in the water and mud. The sad scene broke his heart and he cried out to God, 'O God, when will we have a roof over our heads in these campaigns?' Immediately he felt God respond and say to him, 'Trust me for a tent for 10,000 people.'

'But Lord,' he said, 'my pockets are empty.' Again he heard God speak into his heart, clearly and decisively, 'Don't plan with what is in your pockets, plan with what is in mine.' Soaked himself, in the still driving rain, he replied, 'Then, Lord, I will plan like a millionaire!'

As soon as the Swaziland campaign was over, Reinhard phoned firms in Johannesburg to enquire about making a tent for 10,000 people. He was told that such a thing was not feasible, and besides the cost would be formidable, perhaps R100,000.

This shook even Reinhard, and once again he prayed about it. CfaN was growing rapidly and their outgoings were always threatening to outstrip their income. However, the Lord confirmed his earlier promise, and so he began to plan 'like a millionaire'.

The tent was designed and produced by an Italian firm in Milan, while the ancillaries were built locally. Thanks to the growing number of prayer partners, especially in Germany and South Africa, the money came in for this staggering venture, including enough to cover the vehicles, chairs and generator. But it would be another year before it was delivered, and in the meantime the campaigns had to go on.

Chapter 14

The Combine Harvester

As Reinhard considered the vastness of the harvest that God was showing him it seemed that he spoke into his heart, 'The day of the sickle is past, this is the day of the combine harvester.' The 10,000-seater tent then being made was testimony itself of this change of scale in his own ministry. It was huge, and the canvas was yellow; it soon became known simply as 'the Yellow Tent'.

Many were inspired by the new slogan, but the critics complained that 'you don't find combine harvesters in Scripture'. Though hurt at the time, long afterwards Reinhard said with a twinkle in his eye, 'I thought one day I had found one — it was called Paul!'

As the size of the campaigns grew, so did his reputation in the country of South Africa, but two other incidents occurred at this time which also spread the news of his ministry. The first happened during a conference that he was involved in, when he received a phone call asking him to go and pray for a Mrs Dinnie Viljoen who had terminal cancer. He was about to say he was too busy, when he sensed the Holy Spirit say to him, 'I am sending you.' That settled the matter, and he set off, together with Michael Kolisang who had just arrived that morning from Lesotho.

When they picked up the man who had phoned he looked uncomfortable on seeing Michael, explaining that the woman belonged to the Dutch Reform Church, and may not like a black man in her house. Although they hated this situation, it was decided that Michael would stay in the car. On the way to the house, the Lord gave Reinhard a scripture for the lady. It was

Habakkuk 3:17&19, 'Though the fig-tree does not bud and there are no grapes on the vines, though the olive crop fails and the fields produce no food ....' As it appeared so unlikely, negative even, he questioned it, but felt certain that it was from the Lord.

As it happened Mrs Viljoen had earlier been given a tape by a nurse of Reinhard preaching, and Michael featured on the tape. She had prayed that, if it was God's will, this Bonnke and his colleague should pray for her. She had also asked her husband to find her a book on prayer by Andrew Murray, but in error he bought another by Hannah Hurnard, called *Hinds Feet on High Places*, based on Habakkuk 3:17&19.

When they arrived, and she learned that the same Michael Kolisang was at that moment sitting in the car, he was invited in, through the front door, to pray for her. As soon as Reinhard rather nervously shared the scripture he had been given, she showed them the book. This raised their faith, and Reinhard said, 'I am sure God is going to do a miracle.' After prayer, during which Mrs Viljoen saw herself 'standing under a great waterfall', Reinhard and Michael rushed back to their conference. A few days later, she returned to hospital where they gave her three days of tests, and were dumbfounded when no trace of cancer was found.

Her testimony opened doors for her all across South Africa, and God used her to win many to the Lord, and break down walls of religious prejudice. On the first anniversary of her healing Reinhard spoke at a great thanksgiving service at which 400 women attended. It was therefore a shock to them all when a short time later she died. However, in the last year of her life she had accomplished more than in the rest of her life put together. And Reinhard's name became better known.

The second incident featured Mr Kruger, who was dying from leukaemia in a Johannesburg hospital ward. Reinhard and Anni went to pray for him one afternoon, but there being nowhere to park, Anni drove around while Reinhard went in. Mr

Kruger was struggling for breath and obviously very ill. As soon as he saw Reinhard he gasped out, 'Pastor Bonnke, have you got a word from God for me?' Reinhard was moved with compassion, and looking into the sunken eyes, he declared, 'Yes. It is written in Psalm 118:17 that "You shall not die, but live and declare the works of the Lord".'

One afternoon a year later, a visitor strode into Reinhard's office and asked, 'Do you remember me?' Reinhard was defeated. With tears in his eyes the visitor said, 'I am Mr Kruger, the man you prayed for a year ago.' Reinhard leapt to his feet, shouting 'Hallelujah!' as he scanned this healthy face before him.

'As soon as you left,' Mr Kruger explained, 'I called the nurse and told her I was going home. They tried to dissuade me but I insisted. They made me sign a disclaimer form and gave me a load of pills, which I threw away, for God had healed me. Every day I got better, and when I went back for tests they found no trace of leukaemia.'

Later Reinhard said, 'All who pray for the sick will be offered as much discouragement as help. But one thing I know; nobody has found one statement in Scripture against divine healing. I know of no profanity worse than healing the sick in Jesus' name to get rich, or to make a name for oneself, or for the gratification of wielding power.'

'Each healing,' he adds, 'is like a laser beam cutting through the darkness of this world, until the day dawns and Christ shall reign. Until then, we fight the good fight of faith, aided by the mercy of God and the gift of healings.'

During 1977 the team held three major campaigns in South Africa, at Bushbuckbridge, Giyani, and Sibasa. At Bushbuckbridge Richard Ngidi's district prevented the popular Zulu evangelist from attending and Reinhard prayed for the sick himself. There were many miracles, including the instant healing of the crippled and the blind.

The second was at Giyani in a remote region of northeast Transvaal bordering Vendaland and Mozambique. The event began in a school, and moved to the local showground. During the event, Reinhard went into the local post office, where the wide-eyed attendant shared his testimony: 'I was a real heathen. I had nothing to do with Christianity. I was a drunkard and unkind to my wife. Then one night I had a dream in which two men in white told me, "Go to the school. You will be shown the way of life." I went, and I am now a child of God!'

By the end of the campaign a small mountain of discarded crutches and walking sticks made a good photographic testimony for the Christ for all Nations prayer partner report. In one adverse comment someone went so far as to say, 'This is typical of the African people ... they are so absent-minded that they forget to take their crutches home with them. ...' At a later date, in response to this comment, Reinhard retorted, 'A cripple may forget his money, he may even forget his wife or his children ... but when he forgets his *crutches* then surely miracles *must* have happened.' How foolish are those who doubt.

When it was over, Reinhard called to thank the schoolmaster who had lent the facilities, and who told him, 'This campaign was different. The people are not talking about you or Michael Kolisang, they are talking about Jesus.' It was the greatest compliment he could have paid to the evangelist.

The highlight of 1977 was undoubtedly the Sibasa campaign in Vendaland. They had applied for permits, but were given an uncompromising 'no'. In this case, however, Reinhard felt sure that this was simply the devil seeking to close the door. Also, although he is normally a very healthy person, suffering only from tinnitus on occasions, he had gone down with flu and had to take to his bed. During the night he awoke and saw the name 'Sibasa' before him in lights. He took it as a definite confirmation to continue. So he visited the government office concerned and found that the official was a Christian. Permission was soon granted, but only for a ten-day campaign.

When the event began, it was so cold and wet that numbers were down to 200, rising only to 400, but by the second week the rain had stopped and the crowd climbed to 30,000. News of the miracles and conversions raced across the country.

One afternoon when Reinhard was alone praying in his caravan, God told him to go and buy a beautiful gift for the country's President. He had to drive some distance to find something suitable — a fine and lovely vase. It was gift-wrapped and he bore it home, wondering how he was to get it delivered.

On his return he found a message waiting for him. The President wanted to see him at 4 pm! This Holy Spirit guidance thrilled Reinhard and his team. At the residence of the President they found his cabinet and their wives all waiting to meet them. President Mphephu greeted them warmly and said, 'Pastor Bonnke I'm sorry for the problems you encountered. I have heard that God has blessed my nation through you and I have called you because I would like to hear what God has to say to us.'

Reinhard recognised a God-given opportunity and was not ashamed to preach the gospel. At the climax he found himself wondering whether he should abide by protocol, or make an 'altar call'! But he knew in his heart that he had to make an appeal. Facing the leaders of this nation he asked, 'Who wants to give his heart and life to Jesus?' The President himself led the way, and his ministers followed. What a moment for the team, and no wonder the forces of darkness had tried to prevent their coming to Vendaland.

On the final night, 40,000 crammed into the stadium. The tide of blessing and the impact on South Africa were beginning to tell.

The Battle Intensifies

The year 1978 saw the opening of the new offices, and the arrival of the Yellow Tent. Its terrific size, far bigger than any circus tent, created tremendous interest in the rapidly expanding team of Christ for all Nations. The final cost was a massive R200,000, double the amount first mentioned, but the Lord covered it.

The first outing to Seshengo, Pietersburg was an outstanding success, making for an atmosphere of security, knowing that they were no longer subject to the fickle elements, or so it seemed.

The tent was then transported on giant trucks to Njele, Vendaland, the convoy causing a great stir of interest everywhere. The raising of it was an advertisement in itself, with its seven-ton masts and huge cables. Everyone was excited.

Njele was a remote town in the shadow of a mountain notorious for its association with demons and departed spirits. A local pastor told them of a missionary who had erected a tent on the same spot, but before he could hold a single meeting a hurricane had ripped it to shreds. The team were not worried.

Within a few days, however, a huge wind and torrential rain transformed the site into a quagmire. One service was abandoned as the safety of the crowd was threatened. Part of the roof tore, and the masts were in danger of collapsing. That night one mast did collapse, and the tent filled with water, having to be slit to prevent the whole structure being destroyed. It was a catastrophe, and although Reinhard was not surrendering, neither was he winning. God supplied the necessary spark of faith through a local Elijah.

Elijah Mulawudzi had been saved in the previous campaign in Vendaland, and he came and sought Reinhard out. With all the enthusiasm of a new believer he said, 'Pastor, didn't you preach that all things are possible to them that believe?' It was just what Reinhard needed to hear. He felt rebuked and stimulated at the same time.

'Yes, you are right,' he said. 'I did preach it, and I do believe it.' As he spoke, his faith lifted, and he took up the challenge. He called together his bedraggled army and told them, 'In the name of Jesus we are going to stay and preach the gospel.'

Within a short time the rain ceased, the sun came out, and the whole scene changed. People came until the tent overflowed. President Mphephu attended one of the closing meetings, and as Reinhard prayed for people to be baptised in the Holy Spirit he watched in amazement as some 1,500 seekers were swept off their feet by the power of God, and began to speak in tongues. God had once again brought triumph out of disaster, through the faith of a new believer.

Back from a preaching tour in Germany, Reinhard pressed on with campaigns in South Africa at Namakgale, Phalaborwa; Mabopane, Pretoria and Acornhoek in Greenvalley. Here the tentmaster had phoned Reinhard to say that the site was poor. If it rained, the tent would collapse. Reinhard told him, 'I tell you in the name of Jesus, it is not going to rain.'

Then in the middle of the seventeen-day campaign disaster threatened as a great storm could be seen brewing over the mountains. The wind was rising and it was all too clear they were right in its path. The black clouds rolled towards them and as the wind tugged at Reinhard's hair, the Holy Spirit spoke: 'Rebuke the devil.'

Reinhard shouted, 'Devil, if you destroy this tent, I am going to trust God for one three times as big.' Before his very eyes the storm clouds parted and passed widely on either side of the tent, without touching the tent area. Later, Reinhard realised he had made a mistake, and full of faith declared, 'Devil, I do not make any deals with you. The big tent comes anyway.' Thus was birthed the vision of the tent which was to catch the eyes of the world.

But as the conflict became hotter, God made Reinhard realise the need to increase his prayer support. The war to win Africa was intensifying, and every campaign was turning into a real battle where the team were learning the secrets of spiritual warfare, proving for themselves that Jesus had given them power over all the power of the enemy.

Witchcraft abounds in Africa, and there can be no compromise between the cross and the occult. Reinhard's uncompromising preaching brought him into open conflict with Satan and the powers of darkness. In some early campaigns he acknowledges he wasted a lot of time running from one demonised person to the next. But under the guidance of the Holy Spirit he realised the diversionary tactics of the devil. Often scores of demons would manifest as soon as he began to preach. But there were thousands who needed to hear the word, so he began to train workers to gather up the demonised and take them away to set them free where they wouldn't disturb the crowd. With typical directness he says, 'We are not there to put on demonstrations, but to preach the gospel.'

Cases of converted witch-doctors and delivered people are many, but Reinhard was not a demon-chaser. 'The word of command should be all that is needed in most cases, as we see in the New Testament instances of deliverance.' He refused to be diverted from his great commission of preaching the gospel, which alone can deal with the root problem of sin. To similar issues which sought to distract him from his God-given vision, he retorted, 'We cannot stop the combine harvester to catch a mouse!'

Satanists came into the meetings and tried to put spells on him, but in vain. One confessed that on one occasion the demons raced around the outside of the tent, but could not enter because it was encircled with a wall of fire.

On another occasion, Michael Kolisang prayed for a young woman who suffered from dumbness. Seeing a witchcraft necklace upon her he cut it, and she began to sing. She went round the villages testifying and in just over a week she led thirty people to Christ.

In the second Soweto campaign in 1981, the conversion of the chief witch-doctor, sixty-six year-old Pauline Mbatha who had 'ruled' the area for ten years, caused a sensation. She walked to the front in her full regalia and said, 'I want all this cut off.' It was burned and the photo of the bonfire in the press stirred Soweto.

This destruction of charms and witchcraft items became an important feature of Reinhard's ministry. The bonfires were a symbol of the victory of the Lord Jesus Christ over Satan and his demons. Sometimes live snakes and even firearms were thrown onto the platform, often to the alarm of the guests there.

Reinhard has said, 'In some areas, especially in Africa, demons are a daily reality, and I find myself on a daily battlefield.' On these battlefields, particularly where Satanism has been entrenched for centuries, constant victory demanded a consistent prayer commitment. From the beginning a growing team of intercessors had supported the ministry. But at this time, when the work was expanding rapidly, God spoke to Reinhard through a dream in which he saw a large warship in danger of being bogged down in a narrow part of a river. The message was clear: without more prayer support, the growing work would founder. Reinhard took the message to heart and enlisted more intercessors. 'Evangelism without intercession is like dynamite without a detonator,' he declared, adding, 'and intercession without evangelism is the detonator without the dynamite.'

He also recruited members of his team into full-time intercession. In 1980, Suzette Hattingh who had been involved part-time in two campaigns became full-time. Her growing understanding in later years would give her an international platform through her teaching on prayer and intercession, but in these early days she was still learning step by step.

The team developed a prayer strategy for the campaigns. Usually the organisers would divide the city into regions, and in the weeks before the event, Suzette or her co-workers would visit each region, teaching and motivating the believers there to become prayer warriors. Then during the event itself, this team would begin to pray an hour or so before the beginning of each meeting, continuing throughout the preaching until the altar call was made. When this programme of specific intercession was introduced there was a marked increase in the miraculous, in the size of the crowds, and the numbers responding to the appeal.

Fasting was a regular feature of these meetings, and of the life of the team. Prompted by the Holy Spirit, Suzette fasted for fifteen days when she joined the team, and subsequently has been led to fast for twenty, thirty and even forty days. Reinhard himself has also fasted for forty days. He says, 'I never knew that I would be able to fast for that long, but then I had such a God-given burning desire to do it that the forty days just slipped by.' He continued, 'The real basis for fasting is throwing ourselves into the business of intercession, an articulation of God-inspired desire. Otherwise it is just a hunger strike. Fasting may be from food. Isaiah and Jeremiah say that the fasting God wants is from sin. If Christians, weeping before God, gave up their self-indulgent habits and resolved to leave alone their greed, or their jealousy, gossiping, pride or uncleanness for even a week, it would be far more effective than missing dinner every night.'

This constant intercession was one of the great secrets behind the way in which the hand of God could be clearly seen in the progress of Christ for all Nations over these years, and God answered many prayers for the protection of the team.

When, a few years later, in 1983 Reinhard was preaching in America, others of the CfaN team were conducting a campaign in the Yellow Tent at Tafelkop in northern Transvaal. The campaign was over but the follow-up team were conducting nightly classes for the new believers. One evening when about 3,000 were present, suddenly a fierce tornado struck the tent. The tent crew immediately took safety precautions but the wind was so violent that they evacuated the tent. Suzette was on the platform and says she never saw people move so quickly; 'I'm sure the angels helped get them out! A mast twisted and collapsed and the one above the platform where I was standing bent like a bow. The organist did a somersault over the edge and disappeared into the night. Moments later I was left with nothing but the automatic beat of the electronic organ.' One or two were trapped, but no one was hurt. When the damage was surveyed the next day it was agreed that it was nothing short of miraculous, especially as there were many women and children present. It would take two months to repair.

In 1978 and 1979 the Yellow Tent tramped around South Africa, but Reinhard was burning to spread his wings. The opportunity came in 1980, when they crossed the famous Limpopo into Zimbabwe. Previously he had turned down urgent invitations from pastors there, even when they had booked a stadium, which pressurised him considerably. Now he was so sure it was God's time that he allocated five months to this great nation. Meetings were planned for several locations with two major campaigns in Harare and Bulawayo. The team had sent an advance party to assist preparation and this thoroughness was rewarded. Three thousand responded on the opening night in Harare — the biggest single response they had seen. After three nights the Yellow Tent overflowed, and they moved to the stadium, despite the chilly weather.

It was a special joy for Reinhard to have with them his father, now aged seventy-five, lovingly known as 'Opa'. One night Hermann had a dream which he quickly shared. 'Reinhard, last night I had a dream in which I saw the tent empty. I am worried that something is wrong.' Reinhard reassured him, 'Your dream is true. Tonight we move to the stadium, because of the crowds!'

On the final night almost 20,000 filled the stadium, and when Reinhard gave the invitation to receive the baptism of the Holy Spirit 5,000 pressed to the front, and again many were prostrated and praised God in other tongues.

In Bulawayo, television and radio gave the campaign generous coverage, and Reinhard appeared on TV several times. By these means, the whole country felt the impact of the campaigns and it was further vindication of Reinhard's commitment to mass evangelism in Africa. The readiness of the people of Zimbabwe to hear the gospel was an indicator that the wind of God was blowing across the continent. The slogan 'Africa shall be saved!' was becoming a real possibility.

If anything, the five campaigns in Zambia the following year were even greater. The campaigns in Livingstone and Lusaka stirred the nation. The press gave them prominence and television featured the meetings and the preaching of the gospel. It finally resulted in Reinhard and his team receiving an invitation to meet and speak with the President, Kenneth Kaunda, in the State House.

By now the team were firmly established on the campaign trail, and in 1982 the team returned to South Africa for nine events across the nation. But with the North calling ever stronger, Reinhard paid a brief visit to Zaire and the way was prepared for future visits to this tremendous nation in the heart of the continent.

Yonggi Cho invited him to visit his church in Seoul, Korea, and the humility and faith of the leader of the world's largest church was a further inspiration to Reinhard to believe for even bigger things, strengthening his resolve to press on with the vision God had given him.

In September, the 13th World Pentecostal Conference was convened for the first time in Africa, in Nairobi, and Reinhard addressed one of the great open air services in Uhuru (Freedom) Park. Thousands streamed to the front for salvation, restoration and healing.

A further extension to Reinhard's international ministry was seen as he began the year 1983 in Perth, Western Australia. These meetings were soon followed by a ten-day campaign in Auckland, New Zealand, and later in May he had an outstandingly successful campaign in Helsinki, capital of Finland, with 10,000 people filling the local ice stadium night after night.

But the pressure of campaigns in Africa continued to grow, for millions were dying without Christ. The year finished with thirteen major events completed. Every year his schedule grew heavier, and to list the commitments and the results leaves one breathless. Numbers which a few years previously had seemed impossible became a regular feature of the campaigns. Again and again, the Yellow Tent was proving too small for the crowds.

But in August that same year another great project was coming to its climax; one which would change the ministry of Reinhard Bonnke for ever. The vision of the Big Tent which had stirred in Reinhard's mind five years earlier was about to be launched. It was to be the highlight of the year.

Chapter 16

The Big Tent

The size of the 'Big Tent' staggered everyone involved in its making: the designers, the manufacturers, the technicians, and especially the cost accountants! The cold statistics were chilling: it covered 12,000 square metres (three acres); the twelve steel masts, each 27 metres high, and which supported the tensioned structure, weighed 5 metric tons each; the fabric weighed 22 tons; and there was 5 kilometres of steel cable. The only person who was not staggered was Reinhard Bonnke.

From the moment he was fully persuaded that God was leading him to make a tent to seat 30,000 people, he was single-mindedly committed to the project and nothing and no one could deflect him, though more than one tried. 'Some people have wishes. Others, like Joshua the son of Nun, have purposes,' he answered his critics. In fact he remembered his disappointment when he discovered that the Yellow Tent could not in fact seat the 10,000 he had planned. It transpired that the designers' faith could not stretch to that capacity and they had 'under-designed' it. Reinhard was determined not to be caught twice, and ordered a tent for 34,000, to allow, as he put it, 'for any hidden doubts among the design team'!

The production of this mighty structure proved no easy task and nothing seemed straightforward. It was the biggest tent of its kind in the world and so there was no precedent. Even the leading designer, J. J. Swanepoel, underestimated the size of the engineering feat. Reinhard thought it could be done in eighteen months, and each year thereafter he was announcing it would be ready 'next year', but in fact it took five years. They hit so many snags it almost seemed as though someone was breeding them;

they descended upon the tent project like plagues of locusts which consumed money alarmingly, placing Reinhard and his colleagues under immense pressure.

In spite of this the campaigns continued with ever-increasing blessing and Reinhard took more and more burdens upon himself as invitations poured in from around the world. Towards the end of 1980 when the Big Tent project was in serious danger of grinding to a halt due to the ever multiplying problems, God gave Reinhard just the man he needed 'for such a time as this'.

Peter van den Berg came from a family of fourth generation pioneers to Rhodesia (now Zimbabwe). Peter's father had a flourishing motor enterprise and Peter had grown up in the business. A motor and aviation engineer, with business administration skills plus a pilot's licence, life was good, in spite of the internal unrest in his home country during the transition to majority rule and independence.

At the age of twenty-seven he was already married with three children when suddenly he and his wife and family responded to the call of God to sell up and train for the ministry at the Elim Bible College near London, England. Two years later, when they ran out of money, having to trust God and 'live by faith', they proved for themselves that God would supply their every need.

After finishing their studies they formed an evangelistic musical group under the Shona name 'Rufaro' (happy), with which they toured for seven years, and through this they met Reinhard in Birmingham, England, when Reinhard was preaching there. Some time before this, Peter had read about Christ for all Nations and God told him that he was to be a part of this work. After prayer, Peter resolved to wait for God to work on his behalf. That day Reinhard spoke to Peter but told him that, for the moment, he really was not looking for preachers but he was urgently in need of a transport manager. To Reinhard's surprise Peter said he would be very happy to accept. During his time at college Peter once said to his wife that he wondered why all his experience and training as an engineer and business manager appeared to be wasted years — now he was to prove otherwise! They returned to Africa and joined CfaN on the 1st January 1981.

The timing was perfect. When he arrived at Witfield it was to find considerable tension as the Big Tent was undergoing the early part of its construction and they were experiencing very complicated technical problems, besides having lost some key personnel. Peter quickly instituted new systems which increased the efficiency of the growing organisation, and within three months Reinhard made him his chief co-ordinator, and ultimately general manager.

A large factory had been obtained at a nearby place called Springs, and it was here that much of the assembly work on the tent was done. Peter's engineering skills were stretched to the limit, but his pioneering spirit revelled in it. With top international consultations in the USA and Italy, wind trials, redesigning, as well as teaching, preaching and singing, every bit of experience he had gained was used to the full.

Over the years Peter and Reinhard have become very close. Peter admires Reinhard's 'simplicity in listening to the Holy Spirit'. He confirms what others have said about Reinhard, that 'what you see is what you get'.

Both Peter and Reinhard have a liking to get things done, and of course Reinhard likes immediate results! When planning for the future, they will often discuss some new proposition and pray about it. Then perhaps three or four days later it is quite common for Reinhard to come to Peter and tell him, 'The Holy Spirit spoke to me in a dream last night about our plans. Now the dream has made it clear and this is what we are going to do. ...' Once Reinhard has made that decision he then runs with it without another doubt about it.

The tent factory soon needed to be enlarged to cope with the work: welding the special steel-work and gluing the computer-patterned panels from America. The first test run was made at the end of 1982 when six of the giant masts were erected with a section of the roof fabric. Reinhard was reduced to tears when he saw the masts raised into position — even the bare masts made a spectacular sight. Hundreds of prayer partners gathered around the steel masts and prayed that the remaining obstacles would be overcome. The test run revealed the need for further modifications; and all the time money was being gobbled up. However, Reinhard was adamant that they were not to take a bank loan. He believed that God had spoken very clearly to him about this and insisted, 'God's instructions are holy to me.' Great sacrifices were made by all involved; the CfaN workers at one period even returned their salaries.

Despite the great financial needs, Reinhard finds it hard to appeal for money. At this time he visited Canada, and David Mainse invited him to appear on his TV programme *100 Huntley Street*. For four days, film of Reinhard and CfaN's work was beamed out across Canada creating tremendous interest. Reinhard was then given the chance to make an appeal to the Christians of Canada, but instead he simply asked, 'Pray for me, pray for our ministry and pray for the lost souls of Africa.' Afterwards a thought flashed into his mind, 'You fool, why didn't you ask them to pay not pray?' But he dismissed this unworthy thought and believed he had done the right thing. Then, unprompted, David Mainse himself appealed for support for Reinhard's work and raised $35,000 for CfaN.

It reminded Reinhard again of an incident that had occurred just as he was starting to reach out to Africa with the vision of CfaN. A woman phoned and made Reinhard a fantastic offer of financial support for his ministry. Reinhard and Anni, young missionaries with three young children, Freddy, Susi and Gabi, having launched out in faith to follow the vision God had given them and no longer being supported officially by the German Fellowship, were now receiving this fabulous offer. Reinhard and Anni went to this lady's home and found it magnificent, reflecting her exceptional wealth. She told Reinhard that she had been watching his ministry for some time and wanted to finance his gospel campaigns in Africa. The amounts mentioned were awesome, beyond their wildest dreams.

To convince them of her ability to fulfil the offer she showed them files of her various assets, including a diamond mine, iron ore deposits, and more. She told him she wanted to form a trust and give half her assets to the work of God and she asked Reinhard if he would like to join the trustees. It was an amazing offer but Reinhard felt a reticence in his spirit. He thanked her and asked if he could pray about it before deciding. Afterwards he found that Anni also had no witness in her heart about it. They prayed and got on with their campaigns.

Then one night he had a frightening dream in which he was crossing a river at dusk. The water was low and a small man invited him to follow him across. Halfway over, a huge hippopotamus rose up before him, then another appeared behind him, then more arose from the mud until he was surrounded by hippos with their gaping jaws threatening him. He cried out, 'Jesus, help me!' That nightmare of a dream was still fresh in his mind when the rich lady phoned him pressing for a decision about the trust fund.

Reinhard and Anni paid her a second visit. She welcomed them warmly and started to show them around the grounds of her mansion. Eventually she brought them to a part where there was a river, and Reinhard was shocked to see that it was identical to the river of his nightmare. Now he understood: there was hidden peril here. He felt the Lord's presence near him and he knew that soon he would have an answer to his prayer for guidance. In the house Reinhard asked if they could pray together. As he knelt he heard the voice of the Lord not once, but three times, saying, 'Have nothing to do with this.' Politely but firmly he thanked the lady for her offer but told her he must decline it. He realised that he must continue to rely on the Lord and felt that he had just passed an important test. He knew that as long as he was obedient in preaching the gospel, God would supply every need, no matter how large.

The Big Tent was now capturing the imagination of people worldwide and becoming news not only in the Christian press but in the international media. In August 1983 the massive structure was raised at a site called KwaThema at Springs near Johannesburg for a test-run campaign. The very size of the tent drew gasps of astonishment from everyone who saw it and the event drew crowds of many thousands, of whom 8,000 made decisions, the 'first fruits' of a far greater harvest to come. The dedication of the Big Tent was planned for February 1984, but one thing still causing them great concern was the need for transport and this became a matter for special prayer. The cost for the trucks alone was estimated at R1.5 million. Invitations to return to America and Canada for television interviews took Reinhard there in November and December and some very generous donations were forthcoming as a result, from people such as Pat Robertson. On his return via Germany he went to a vehicle depot near Hamburg. There he found vehicles which might have been tailor-made for the Big Tent — they were six-wheel drive trucks, fitted with hydraulic winches, especially strengthened for North African conditions. These brand new trucks had been built for the army of Colonel Gadaffi of Libya but were now surplus to his requirements and Reinhard was able to purchase them at half-price! All that needed to be done was to re-spray them and paint the CfaN logo on them. Truly swords had been turned into ploughshares.

After five years of struggle, everything was now ready for the great dedication day of the Big Tent, to be followed by a two-week campaign in Soweto. Determined not to miss this unique occasion, they came by the plane load from Germany, America, Finland, Britain and Australia; they came by bus and by car from all over South Africa; and by bicycle and on foot from all over Johannesburg.

Saturday, 18th February dawned a perfect day. Forty thousand rejoicing people packed the world's biggest tent to overflowing, with many standing, row after row. There was a praise festival in the morning, and the dedication service was scheduled for 4 pm, by which time the flaps were lifted so that the thousands outside could watch and hear. Some estimated that, finally, there were 50,000. Many denominations were represented in a beautiful display of Christian unity. The veteran Zulu evangelist, Nicholas Benghu, offered the dedication prayer, along with Revd Paul Schoch from the USA. The climax of the day came when 5,000 people responded to Reinhard's appeal to accept Jesus Christ as Saviour, pouring forward into the now dwarfed Yellow Tent for follow-up counselling and prayer, a river of people flowing from hell into heaven.

The two-week long Soweto campaign which followed was an outstanding success; night after night thousands came forward for salvation and healing, including a woman witch-doctor whose son had been praying for her salvation for nine years. By the end of the campaign over 25,000 had responded to the invitation to receive Christ.

The Big Tent attracted world wide media attention. An American TV crew spent weeks making a full-length documentary film for the Christian TV network in the USA. A BBC news team also visited the campaign and their filmed report was shown on the main news programmes in the UK, Australia, Zimbabwe and other countries. For once a Christian news item was grabbing the headlines and hundreds of millions saw the gospel attracting tremendous crowds and that miracles were still happening in 1984.

Reinhard's vision to preach the gospel from Cape Town to Cairo led them to plan the next campaign in Cape Town in May of the same year, on the Valhalla Park Sports Field. The very transporting and raising of the tent there fuelled the faith of the churches supporting the campaign. Five thousand had trained as counsellors, and 1,500 as ushers and stewards. Thousands had been praying for months, believing that God was going to pour out his Spirit on Cape Town, with thousands being saved.

Meanwhile, Reinhard had accepted an invitation to preach at the Full Gospel Businessmen's Fellowship International Conference in Singapore. The return flight presented him with the opportunity of a four-day visit to his sister Felicitas, a nurse, and now married to Dr Ron Shaw, both of whom were working with Mark Buntain's hospital in Calcutta. It was a family visit and he had not anticipated preaching but when he arrived he found that they had laid on a four-day campaign for him. He hadn't the heart to refuse.

On a previous visit to his sister he had been warned beforehand that this needy city had gained a reputation of being 'the graveyard for great evangelists'. He had replied, 'Well, I don't have to worry ... I'm not a great evangelist. ' During the four days of this second visit, at least 4,000 answered the salvation appeals. The majority of those attending were Hindus but as he does in Africa, Reinhard encouraged the new believers to get rid of their various charms which adorned their arms, necks and waists. A leading minister in the city said it was the first time he had seen any evangelist challenge the people to break away from their superstitious trinkets. They responded and in obedience people cut them off and threw them onto the platform. Handfuls were collected each night and burned. Outstanding healings were witnessed of the blind and lame.

In the midst of all this God spoke to Reinhard and told him, 'The tent is destroyed.' It was two days later before news at last reached him. But God had already given him peace in his heart — so much so in fact that Reinhard said to his wife, 'Anni, I'm worried that I am not worried!' The 'peace of God that passes all understanding' continued to 'garrison' his heart and mind on the long flight back to Africa. During those few days he was probably the only one with any semblance of peace.

In Cape Town everyone was devastated by the disaster — nobody knew what to do. One thing only seemed certain: the great Cape Town campaign would have to be cancelled. It looked as though the bold venture to carry the gospel the full length of Africa from Cape to Cairo was doomed to perish 'on the starting block'. Christians were in tears, asking, 'Why has God allowed this ... ?' The sceptics gloated. The only bit of good news was that no one had been hurt. For those on the spot, the situation was made even worse because the two key men were out of the country at the time — Reinhard in India, and Peter in America.

On his return, Reinhard surveyed the scene. The once proud, giant steel masts now stood as though embarrassed at the naked spectacle they presented to the crowds of gaping sightseers, fully exposed to all after the cruel winds had shamelessly ripped off their million-dollar covering dress, piece by piece, leaving only the tattered shreds to slap mockingly around their battered tops. What had gone wrong?

On Saturday, 5th May, shortly after the tent had been safely erected in spite of a few problems with rain and wind, a few rips appeared in the roof fabric but they were quickly repaired. By evening, however, the wind freshened again and the technicians made further safety checks but felt reassured as the main anchors which were concreted in were holding firm. There was no danger there, and tests during construction had shown that the tent was well able to cope with winds of up to 120 mph.

The night security patrols reported all to be well until the early hours of Sunday morning. Around 4 am the wind suddenly became a roar, and within minutes the tent crew were out in force. Everything seemed all right at first — the steel cables were secure, but then they heard the slaps, and could see material flapping in the wind as a panel was starting to tear. By 7:30 am, the rips were getting larger. The next two hours were a nightmare as the crew were forced to stand helpless and watch the wind tear away thousands of square metres of fabric, peeling it off strip after strip. By 9:30 am the rape was over, tattered remains of canvas hanging like washing from the huge stays. Some of the toughest members of the crew were reduced to tears and wept until they could weep no more. Five years of toil had perished in five hours.

When the campaign committee met that evening, their faces would have graced any gathering of undertakers. For nine months they had planned with unprecedented unity among the city's churches, and their hopes had never been brighter. Now they felt as though they had lost a baby. Then Pastor Dave Onions stood to prophesy, and the anointing pierced through their depression like a shaft of radiance from the throne room of heaven: 'My glory shall be the canopy that covers the people, and the praises of my people shall be the pillars.'

Everyone present felt an immediate witness in their hearts that this was truly a word from the Lord. They decided that the campaign must go ahead and that it should be at the Valhalla Park Sports Ground. The weather could present a problem at that time of year in Cape Town, but in view of the prophecy they decided in faith to stay at the present site.

Reinhard's return did much to restore their spirits. As they stood beneath the bare masts of the wrecked tent they prayed and praised God, trusting God to turn the disaster into a bigger victory than ever. There was a tremendous 'prayer recoil' within the city.

Their prayers were answered. The weather became unseasonably warm and dry for the whole campaign, and the crowds grew to 70,000, far bigger than the tent could have held. Best of all, during the eighteen days of the campaign, a record 29,000 people were counselled after making a commitment to the Lord. At the end of the event, the platform was littered with discarded wheelchairs and unwanted crutches, no longer required by those whom the Lord had healed.

But already Reinhard was planning beyond the Big Tent for something entirely new which had been forming in his heart for some months — a great conference to bring together hundreds of evangelists from all over Africa. His experience with men like Michael Kolisang on his own team and the Zulu evangelist, Richard Ngidi, as well as the hundred bicycle colporteur evangelists he had used in the first Soweto outreach, had made him appreciate their gifted and anointed ministries. His travels had made him realise the tremendous potential of the many hundreds of evangelists who were scattered all over Africa, many of them in remote and lonely places, and so poor they had little chance of ever attending a conference. 'Africa shall be saved' was his watchword, but he knew that it was not for him alone. If only they could be brought together for a special conference, a Fire Conference, that was it! In spite of the impossible financial situation he was in after constructing the Big Tent, he committed himself to this new concept because he recognised that this was the leading of God.

However, it would be another two years before that vision would come to fruition.

Chapter 17

The Ultimate Price

After Cape Town the original plan was for two more campaigns in 1984 in South Africa with the Big Tent, at Durban in August, and in the capital city of Pretoria in November. The tent was insured and there were early hopes that a new tent roof would be delivered in a matter of months, but all too soon it became apparent that the insurance claim was not going to be settled quickly, nor without a great deal of wrangling.

The destruction of the Big Tent could so easily have proved disastrous for Reinhard and Christ for all Nations. After the campaign, although the churches in Cape Town were bulging with new believers, there was no shortage of questions or critics of the Big Tent project. However, the real answers would have to wait until 'we shall know even as we are known', in heaven. One thing was certain: it is faith which turns disasters into triumphs, and losses into gains.

The vast crowds which gathered under the open sky and around the bare masts in Valhalla Park in Cape Town fired Reinhard's vision to still greater heights. It was the first time that they had reached as many as 70,000 in one meeting. Already he was sensing new possibilities. God could turn this terrible 'set-back' into a tremendous step forward.

Just as Paul was able to write from his prison cell in Rome, 'What has happened ... has really served to advance the gospel' (Philippians 1:12), so ultimately the destruction of the tent roof served to advance the impact of CfaN on the whole of the African continent. Despite the enormous cost and apparent waste, the building and destruction of the largest tent in the world was news. The ministry of CfaN became international almost overnight, and Reinhard became known throughout the world as 'the man who built the Big Tent'. Though he may not have known it at the time, Cape Town was to be the last major campaign he was to hold in South Africa, the country to which he had first been called.

Meanwhile, the programme of campaigns was changed and instead of Durban and Pretoria it was decided to return to Zimbabwe. A week in Bulawayo in October 1984 recorded an aggregate attendance of 50,000 with close on 10,000 decisions. In November, a sixteen-day campaign in the capital Harare on the local show grounds saw crowds of up to 35,000 attending and Reinhard noticed a definite up-swing in the spiritual climate in the country since their 1980 campaign there. This was borne out by the response, the aggregate attendance being around 300,000 and the number of decisions 31,000 — higher even than Cape Town.

During a visit to America Reinhard, with his South African friend, Pastor Ray McCauley, went to Dallas where they were invited out to dinner by Kenneth and Gloria Copeland. Ray and Reinhard had been discussing the problem of replacing the tent roof because of the delay in the insurance claim being settled. As they sat down for the meal, Kenneth Copeland asked Reinhard to tell them exactly what had happened to the tent. After hearing his story, Kenneth Copeland said, 'The Lord told me to pay for a new tent roof.' It was a staggering offer because the cost was estimated at US$800,000. For once, Reinhard could hardly believe his ears. The offer was even more incredible because at that particular time Kenneth Copeland's own ministry was experiencing financial problems of its own. But true to his word the cheque was forthcoming, enabling the new tent roof to be ordered from a company in Bath, England, who were also instrumental in getting it put into the *Guinness Book of Records*. When the final account was settled there was a balance of US$20,000. Reinhard was going to return it to Kenneth

Copeland but he generously insisted that Reinhard retain it for his next campaign.

The year of 1984, which had seen the dedication and destruction of the Big Tent, also saw the greatest harvest of any year up to that time, with more than 150,000 souls responding to the call for salvation — a true vindication, if one was needed, of the Lord's blessing on the whole project.

The next year, 1985 was another exceedingly busy one. The famine situation which was causing much suffering across wide areas of Africa provoked Reinhard and his team into another new venture, 'Bread for Africa'. A special fund and separate banking account were set up for this, and two of the giant trucks normally used for transporting the Big Tent were used to carry eighty tons of maize meal, along with clothing and Bibles, to Mozambique where the famine was exacting a terrible toll. Aid was also given to feed children in some of the poorest areas in Zimbabwe.

The call to reach out across this great continent was tugging ever more strongly at his heart and at the beginning of 1985, Reinhard decided that, accompanied by Peter van den Berg, it was time to reconnoitre some of the West African nations. Like Joshua and Caleb of old, they returned with a good report of the possibilities of record harvests of souls in nations such as the Ivory Coast, Togo, Ghana and Nigeria.

During their visit to Nigeria they met Archbishop Benson Idahosa at his headquarters in Benin City and he invited Reinhard to share with him in a campaign in the strongly Muslim city of Ibadan in March. This city, with a population of around four million people, had proved very resistant to the gospel, and Benson Idahosa was hopeful that by joining forces they might yet make an impact. Neither of them could have foreseen the response they received. The venue was the Olubadan Sports Stadium and the size of the crowds staggered everyone, especially the police who had to deal with the resulting traffic jams.

The local newspaper, *The Daily Sketch*, reported, 'The Olubadan Stadium was packed full inside and outside. Never in the history of the Nigerian Federation had people gathered in such large numbers for such an occasion. Not even the visit of Queen Elizabeth of Great Britain to Nigeria, or the historic Independence Day, or any political rally has attracted such an indescribable meeting of heads for a single purpose — to be healed and re-created.'

Some newsmen reckoned there were up to half a million at one gathering, and Reinhard confessed, 'The size of the gathering was something my eyes have never seen before.' The two evangelists, Benson Idahosa and Reinhard, alternated the preaching between them and it worked remarkably well. Although both of them are first and foremost evangelists, they are very different personalities. Nevertheless together they reaped a rich harvest, and saw God confirm his word with signs and wonders. The *Evening Sketch* gave details of some of the many healings: 'Adebisi Adeyemi, paralytic — started walking and jumped happily on the rostrum. Justina Olu Olaji, of Ile-Ife, had been blind for twenty-five years, regained his sight. For seven years Aminatu Oladele was a deaf mute, but heard and spoke a few words.' The Nigerian campaign was a foretaste of the still greater things which lay ahead.

Reinhard and Peter learned something else during their West African visit. The current political climate throughout most of the continent had become totally antagonistic to the apartheid regime in South Africa and anything South African was considered evil. If gospel tracts had 'Printed in South Africa' written on them, they would be instantly discarded. Reinhard and Peter had only managed to enter Nigeria because one was German, and the other Zimbabwean. Had either held South African passports, they would never have been given visas.

So although he held a very successful meeting in Pretoria in April/May 1985, in the very bastion of Afrikanerdom and South Africa's political heart, where he saw many thousands of blacks, whites, coloureds and Indians together in an outstanding display of unity, Reinhard was beginning to ask himself, 'Has the time come to leave South Africa?' Such a huge decision required much careful thought and prayer before sharing it with anyone.

Not all African nations were closed to them however, and other campaigns were already lined up for the remainder of the year. In August they returned to the Matero stadium in Lusaka in Zambia for a sixteen-day campaign. One of the persistent questions which evangelists have to face is that of the fruit — does it last? Now they had an opportunity to find out, because four years had elapsed since the great campaign in the same stadium in 1981. To their joy they found believers from 1981 everywhere, and they didn't have to search for them.

When Reinhard appeared on Zambia Television he was met by a journalist who told him, 'Four years ago I found Christ as Saviour under your ministry. So did my wife, who at that time was suffering from terrible abscesses for which she could find no medical relief. In the Yellow Tent she received Jesus as Saviour and the abscesses dried up and disappeared and have not troubled her again.' His superior also became a Christian in the 1981 meetings. By the end of the campaign there were thousands more who would link their salvation with the 1985 campaign. Over 18,000 decision cards were completed and daily crowds of around 20,000 attended, which mounted to almost 40,000 at weekends. Many testified to being healed.

The country was so stirred that Zambia Television sent a crew to make a documentary film of CfaN. Heading the ZTV crew was one Frederick Chiluba, who the following year was in Malawi on trade union work when Reinhard was campaigning there. He wanted to receive the power of the Holy Spirit and came to the site, and although Reinhard was not there in person, he found some of his team who prayed for him. Then, in Chiluba's own words, 'Suddenly I was carried away in some kind of tongue I couldn't understand. I was overjoyed.' In 1991 this same Frederick Chiluba won a landslide victory to become the President in the country's first ever democratic elections and declared Zambia a Christian nation.

From Zambia, Reinhard moved into the great nation of Zaire for a campaign in Lubumbashi, formerly known as Elizabethville before Zaire gained its independence from Belgium in 1960. Zaire is the third largest country on the African continent with a population in excess of forty million. This nation, deep in the tropical heart of Africa, had seen a succession of missionary pioneers who had struggled at great cost to spread the gospel in the last 150 years. David Livingstone, Henry Stanley, C.T. Studd, Willie Burton, James Salter — the list is endless — have all played their part.

In 1960 a terrible blood-bath followed on the heels of Independence in which thirty-one evangelical missionaries were martyred, as well as hundreds of Zairian pastors, and many thousands of believers. Lubumbashi was the scene of some of the fiercest fighting during those years and twenty years later Reinhard found that the scars were still not fully healed. But the church had withstood the fiercest opposition that Satan could muster against it, and was still alive. The brief five-day campaign revealed the potential as well as the problems of this unique nation.

The stadium was filled with crowds of up to 75,000 people and as many as 10,000 decisions at each meeting overwhelmed the counsellors who just could not cope with such a response. As Reinhard and Michael Kolisang prayed for the sick, many deaf and blind people testified to being healed, and especially notable was the healing of two crippled children, a ten-year-old boy and nine-year-old girl. The boy demonstrated his healing to the vast crowd by jumping up and down like a yo-yo, while the girl could not stop running around — she was so thrilled to find she could now run.

An historic breakthrough was made in Lubumbashi when three of the meetings went out live on television and radio, which meant that several million more people saw and heard through the electronic media. In addition, Reinhard and two of his team appeared on a TV chat show one evening. People phoned in to say that they had been saved or healed through the television and radio transmissions.

It was not all straightforward, however, and Reinhard was very conscious that lots of things were 'different' in Zaire. Many of the children were quite wild and ill-disciplined, there was much extreme poverty, and there was a language barrier. Nevertheless, plans were made to return. Covering the whole continent with the gospel was going to be more demanding and more dangerous than any of them realised. Just how dangerous they were soon to discover.

Even though the Big Tent was idle while awaiting its new roof, the trek to Zambia and Zaire still involved seven of CfaN's large trucks carrying the technical team's equipment, as well as three smaller vehicles. On the long return journey south tragedy struck.

The CfaN convoy of vehicles had just passed through the Zaire border post into Zambia when one of the trucks was involved in a head-on collision with a fuel tanker. Vision was almost totally obscured due to a cloud of dense, white, billowing dust thrown up by a passing truck when the accident occurred.

The driver of the CfaN truck, Horst Kosanke, was killed instantly; his co-driver Milton Kasselman was flung out of the driver's cab by the impact. Milton tried to help Horst but a fuel tank exploded and he died in the flames. The vehicles blazed for six hours. Everything was on fire, even the tar on the road. The driver's cab was melted by the intense heat.

Members of the CfaN team, armed with fire extinguishers, tried to approach the blazing wrecked vehicles but the intense heat drove them back; it was impossible for anyone to get near the cab. A badly injured woman, flung into the road from the other truck, was rescued by two members of the team. They carried her to safety even as the flames from the spilled fuel were racing towards her.

The tragedy was made even more poignant by the fact that Horst's eldest son Rudy, aged just nineteen, witnessed the fiery death of his father. Milton's younger brother, Daniel, was also in the convoy. The stricken CfaN members assembled at the roadside in a sad, shaking huddle of grief, weeping openly as they vainly sought to comfort one another. The 3rd September 1985 was a day none of them would ever be able to forget.

As soon as Reinhard heard, he and Peter van den Berg flew to join his grieving team. It was a terrible time for all of them. Several days later the funeral took place at Witfield. Reinhard reminded the many mourners of a warning which the Holy Spirit had given two years previously: 'Repeatedly, the Spirit said that a time would come when some of us would lay down our lives for the sake of the gospel. The Holy Spirit spoke of martyrdom. The path we are treading is red with the blood of martyrs who have gone before us. But no matter what the price or cost, this vision will find fulfilment. Even if we back out, God will find someone else. But we will go this way until the end, until Jesus comes. The blood of the martyrs is the seed of the church. The more Satan kills the saints, the more God's people prosper, the more the kingdom of God grows.'

With the two coffins before them, draped with the flags of West Germany and South Africa, Reinhard went on to reaffirm his own commitment and to challenge his colleagues: 'We are not backing out from this divine call. If anyone says he cannot pay the price or the road is too rough, I will ask him to rather look for a more comfortable ministry. The road ahead is tough and rough, but at the same time glorious. I for one want to walk it to the end.'

Both of the men were married with families. Horst Kosanke was forty years old, and had joined the team from Germany in August 1983. He and his wife Lydia had two sons, Rudy and Ingemar. Lydia, who was pregnant at the time of the accident, gave birth to their third child, Rebecca, in January 1986, after returning to Germany in December 1985. Milton Kasselman, aged thirty-four, left a wife, Jane, and two children, Linda and Riaan. Milton had been with CfaN for five years.

Reinhard's words were not idle ones, and in the days ahead he and his team would have to flee for their lives during a return visit to Nigeria. In many campaigns he was aware that religious extremists posed a constant threat, admitting that it would only take one bullet. The thought could not be excluded from his mind, but it had been faced and he refused to allow it to stop him preaching the gospel through any door which God had opened to him.

The tragedy left its mark on all of them but it also served to challenge many Christians around the world to a deeper commitment to Christ.

At the end of October 1985 Reinhard returned to West Africa, to visit Accra, Ghana's capital city, for a five-day campaign which, by a last minute switch of venue, had to be held on the local race course. The late change of venue got the meetings off to a slow start with only 20,000 people present on the first night, but on the last night the crowd was estimated at a massive 120,000 people. Close to 70,000 people prayed the prayer of repentance and acceptance of Jesus during the five days. There were many outstanding healings and the whole city was stirred. The local pastors were absolutely delighted and arrangements were made for return visits to Ghana. West Africa had opened its arms to the ministry and Reinhard saw a huge potential harvest there. He longed to be able to bring the weight of the whole team into action to gather it in.

Throughout the early months of 1985, Reinhard had continued to be exercised about the question of leaving South Africa. At the beginning of the year he had been seriously considering expanding the facilities at CfaN's headquarters at Witfield, but he did not feel free to proceed. He sought God in prayer for clear guidance, and step by step he received it. Now he realised that the very location of the ministry in South Africa during these politically turbulent years was a severe hindrance to their ability to spread the gospel across the continent.

Once again God spoke into his heart, 'You must leave South Africa because, "Africa shall be saved!".' Reinhard's first thought was that they would move their base to Kenya. When he returned from the trip to West Africa he called the team together and told them, 'We are leaving South Africa in a year's time. After Harare next year we shall not be returning to Witfield.' The effect of this announcement on his team was as though another tent had just been blown down — there was consternation.

Reinhard himself still did not know whether they should move to Kenya or Europe and so he continued to agonise in prayer. He knew that there was no room for mistakes on such a vital issue. Then one morning he received a phone call from a Christian minister called Johnnie Bosman who said he felt that God had given him a prophecy, although he himself had no idea what it meant.

God had told him to tell Reinhard, 'If you want to jump over a chasm, you cannot do it in two jumps. You have got to do it in one.' Johnnie was perplexed as to what it meant, but not Reinhard, who knew immediately what God was saying to him. The chasm was Africa and they had to move their base to Europe. It was clear to him at last, but he knew instinctively that many South Africans would not understand such a drastic leap and, even more painful, he knew that some of his own team members would not be able to accept it.

As he had anticipated, it proved to be a difficult and painful time for all of them but Reinhard was absolutely certain that this was the will of God and had to be embraced at whatever cost. Events proved that it was the right decision and the timing was perfect. At that time, fifty-five per cent of their support was drawn from South Africa, but once the move to Germany was announced it dropped down almost to zero, although the German support then soared.

Germany was chosen because not only was it Reinhard's native land, but more importantly it was the base of so much of the prayer support. Frankfurt chose itself as a location, having the largest international airport with good access to Africa. They were able to buy an ideal office complex in Frankfurt for one million pounds and it quickly became the nerve centre for the rest of the world as well as the mission centre for Africa. Most of the African members of the team could not come to Frankfurt but all of them worked out their time and other doors opened for them. Reinhard's ministry also flourished as never before. Once again he had dared to march to God's drum beat, even in the face of some opposition and not a little misunderstanding. It soon proved to be easier to get to most African nations by air from Frankfurt than from Johannesburg, and it was certainly easier to move funds in and out of Africa from Frankfurt than from Witfield. The move was to be of even greater significance in later years. While the commitment to the original vision of an Africa washed with the blood of Jesus remained the clear priority, the ministry of Reinhard Bonnke had moved at last from the platform of a continent onto the world stage.

Part Three

Into all the World

Chapter 18

Spreading the Fire

All this time the burden to organise a massive 'Fire Conference' for evangelists from every part of Africa was never far from Reinhard's mind. The death in May 1985 of his good friend and colleague, evangelist Richard Ngidi, only served to fuel his determination to hold this conference. In his tribute to this great Zulu Christian leader, Reinhard said, 'He was a giant in the kingdom of God and a man of faith. It was his faith in the early days of Christ for all Nations that really got me rolling.' The purpose of the Fire Conference was to help get as many African evangelists as possible 'really rolling'.

The strategy behind this conference was a directive of the Holy Spirit to Reinhard, 'Multiply your own ministry.' How? 'Through a conference.' But this was to be a conference with a difference. The objective was to set evangelists on fire and inspire them with faith to fulfil Christ's Great Commission.

While the vision of a blood-washed Africa gripped his heart, the overwhelming enormity of the task made it clear that every hand was needed on deck. 'The church is not a pleasure boat. It is a life boat. There is no room for passengers.' The harvest was so huge that every evangelist was needed. Not only that, but once again God had showed him the divine pattern, evangelism with a demonstration of the power of the Holy Spirit, and he longed to pass this on and see other evangelists equipped with both the zeal and the anointing God had given to him. For he believed passionately that 'evangelism is one on fire setting others on fire'.

With this in mind, Reinhard also decided that this would be more than a conference. He wanted to demonstrate 'fire' evangelism. There would therefore be a gospel campaign at the same time as the conference, so that during the day the evangelists could be taught, and in the evenings they could see the power of God in action. It was to prove to be a divinely inspired concept which would be built upon in later years.

It was settled that this great conference would be held in Harare, Zimbabwe, but twice the provisional dates had to be changed. Originally conceived for the end of 1984, it was moved to 1985, and then postponed further to 1986.

The new roof of the big gospel tent was finally completed in time for the Fire Conference at Harare which took place from 21st to 27th April 1986 under the direction of Chris Lodewyk. The name, For Inter-African Revival Evangelists (FIRE), was not much of a hit but the conference was.

It was a gigantic venture of faith to bring together so many evangelists from every part of Africa, as well as many other parts of the world. Reinhard undertook to sponsor 1,000 evangelists from Africa for the conference — a costly and bold step which would have important repercussions, because nothing was to be done 'on the cheap'. Everything was the best: top speakers were engaged; the magnificent new Harare Sheraton Hotel and Conference Centre was the venue, with an auditorium seating 4,500 delegates. Aircraft were chartered, and the Big Tent, repaired with a shining new white roof, and re-dedicated, was used every evening for a great evangelistic meeting. It was a unique combination of teaching followed by practice.

There were over 4,100 delegates, and forty-one out of the forty-four African countries were represented, as well as delegates from twenty non-African nations. The flags of the African nations hanging around the hall made a magnificent sight. The spiritual atmosphere was electric with anticipation as

Reinhard shared the vision with their eager hearts: 'There has never been a revival without aggressive evangelism. We have only one generation to save this generation. After that it's too late. Yet God's people seem content to see millions of precious human beings die and go to hell. Christ did not die to give people careers. Every single church activity should relate to turning the world back to God. The church that does not seek the lost is lost itself.'

In the evening campaigns in the Big Tent, the platform was shared by several 'international' evangelists, and 8,000 first-time decisions for Jesus were counted, as well as thousands of re-dedications. There were many convincing miracles of healing, including the blind, deaf and cripples.

The lives of the delegates would never be the same. One group of delegates consisted of ten out of a fourteen-strong British Airways crew, five of whom subsequently went into full-time ministry. Pastor Eric Cowley married one of the air hostesses and launched his own ministry in Liberia and other West African countries. There were a thousand similar stories.

Welsh evangelist and singer Ray Bevan testified, 'I had got into automatic pilot. The gift was just carrying me, but there was no fire in it. During the conference something happened inside of me, supernatural.' When he arrived home, 'The difference could be seen already in the first meeting I went to where I was asked to sing. It was a church business meeting, but when I began to speak and sing, men were weeping and falling on the floor.'

But this conference did more than just set on fire 4,000 evangelists. It radically changed the ministry of CfaN, and of Reinhard Bonnke himself. During one of the sessions, American evangelist David Newbury, with the power of God upon him, laid his hands on Reinhard, who dropped to his knees. David Newbury then brought a prophetic word which stunned him with the promise of God's grace:

... and my anointing is upon this man today in a measure that it has been upon no man in this generation. And from among you today I am calling servants that will have the anointing of a thousand, that will raise up and he will be equal to one thousand men with the anointing that I will place upon him.

The Lord will have Reinhard Bonnke to know that the Lord is no more restricting thee, that from this day forth the Lord is giving thee the door-key, the Lord is giving thee the wine, the Lord is giving thee the oil, the Lord is giving thee the abundance of the supply of the harvest. The harvest has come!

This word not only deeply touched the vision of Reinhard, but so stirred the spirits of others in the room, that for many it was the final confirmation that moved them into full-time ministry. Many of them joined the CfaN team after this event. Derek Murray became CfaN's sound engineer; Steve Mutua went on to become the ministries East African director, Gordon and Rachel Hickson became campaign directors, and Rob and Vanessa Birkbeck became international projects and publications managers.

Loren Cunningham, founder of Youth With a Mission, concluded, 'I listened the first night as Reinhard Bonnke said "Africa shall be saved". I heard something beyond a man's voice. I heard the cry of God, the desire of God, but also a statement of faith. It will be done, the promise and fire of God for the continent of Africa. I have watched it over and over again. He lives it, he breathes it. He is living for the day that Africa is saved ... and I believe it will be.'

The commissioning of the Big Tent, the move from Africa to Europe, and the Harare Fire Conference, coming as they did within two years of each other, changed the dimensions of the ministry. From then on Reinhard began to think more and more in global terms. Until then the course of the ministry had followed a fairly linear path, albeit a dramatic one. Thereafter, like a sky-rocket shooting its trail of fire high into the air, it seemed to burst into many separate trails of light.

One trail, of course, had to continue, and that was the African campaigns. But now that the base was moving from South Africa a new strategy was being developed — one that would enable an astonishing number of events to be completed in the next few years.

Invitations from around the world were also pouring in, and despite the clear primary call to Africa, Reinhard was moved with compassion by these cries for help, like Paul's vision of the man of Macedonia in Acts 16:9. After prayer he decided to 'tithe' one event each year outside the continent, and thus the international campaign trail began.

Out of the Fire Conference also was spawned the plan of spreading the fire by literature as well, and Reinhard began to write the book *Evangelism by Fire*, as well as other booklets. The literature trail of the ministry was born, but he never dreamed then where that would subsequently lead him.

When God had called him to 'leap the chasm' into Europe, he had made it clear that it was not just for convenience, but also because God wanted to use CfaN in bringing the gospel message to Europe as well. Reinhard's ministry had developed into one of mass evangelism, a medium which was transparently effective in Africa. However, from his experiences of earlier visits, he knew that he couldn't expect such huge crowds in the prevailing spiritual climate and culture of the European nations. A different strategy was called for, and it was therefore natural to extend the concept of the Fire Conferences. The plan was to have a series spread geographically across Europe to equip the European evangelists in the same manner, another trail called 'Euro-Fire'. Within the next four years three such events were held, in Frankfurt, Germany; in Birmingham, England; and in Lisbon, Portugal.

In the Frankfurt Fire Conference of 1987, 14,000 people, of whom more than 10,000 were German, crowded into the great conference centre. Many had been sponsored to come from Eastern Bloc countries, still at that time under the Soviet Union. They were also given special sets of video tapes to take home, which produced 'mini-Fire Conferences' whenever they were shown, for years afterwards.

There was a tremendous outpouring of the Holy Spirit and many were healed, including a young Swiss girl whose sight was restored. The event exceeded all expectations, especially those of the sceptics who considered this 'African missionary' crazy to hire such a big hall. But as always Reinhard was in too much of a hurry to press on with the gospel flame to stop and argue with his critics. Dr Wolfhard Margies, a respected pastor from Berlin, said, 'Today we speak about our ministries as before or after Euro-Fire '87. Since that time there is a marked difference in the flow of the Holy Spirit.'

The following year Euro-Fire moved to Birmingham, England, in the National Exhibition Centre. Colin Urquhart described it as 'a watershed for Britain'. With over 12,000 delegates, there was a powerful move of unity among the denominations which spread across the nation, and especially Northern Ireland, as pastors returned home 'in the power of the Holy Spirit'.

One of the highlights of the Birmingham conference was the testimony of Mrs Jean Neil of Rugby, England, who had been healed when Reinhard Bonnke had prayed for her a few months earlier in a youth meeting. She had been in a wheelchair for many years, and was completely and instantly healed from numerous ailments. Caught on an amateur video camera, she tentatively rose from her wheelchair, then as her strength returned, she ran around the whole auditorium. She remains fully recovered today.

These conferences were establishing a new benchmark for the urgency of evangelism among church leaders of these

European nations. Both were an important forerunner of a much greater evangelistic effort still to come to these nations.

The 1990 Euro-Fire in Portugal also broke new ground. This Catholic nation has long been considered a spiritual graveyard. But a year of intense preparation produced an event such as Lisbon had never seen. All of these Euro-Fire Conferences maintained the pattern set in Harare of a concurrent evangelistic campaign, and Lisbon was no exception. Before the event, street evangelism and a March for Jesus had primed the population, but with 7,000 delegates and 12,000 in the evening meetings this was both the largest conference and the largest evangelistic campaign in Portugal. The influence spread as far as Greenland and Greece, Morocco and Egypt, all of which sent delegations. One bus-load had come, totally unannounced, all the way from Budapest. The ripples of these events continued long after they were over.

Although the original intention was to have four Euro-Fire Conferences, delegates had been attracted from so far afield to these three that it became clear that God's purpose through them had been fulfilled when the third was over.

After the three Euro-Fire events, Fire Conferences returned to Africa. This time instead of great international events that took much time and huge resources to organise, regional events would be held alongside each and every gospel campaign. The planning of these conferences was now much easier, for volunteers were easy to find. They were the enthusiastic ones, the ones with tears in their eyes, the ones who were filled with Holy Spirit zeal. They were the ones who had been to Harare! In all events after that date the pattern was the same. The fire was spreading.

First came a conference in Kinshasa, Zaire. Then after four years of patiently praying, the door opened in 1993 for a campaign and Fire Conference in the predominantly Muslim city of Dar es Salaam, in Tanzania. Pastors and evangelists came from a score of cities and regions as far away as Kilimanjaro and Zanzibar. A new pattern had emerged. Reinhard thrilled the delegates when he told them, 'God doesn't want a Paul or a Luther or a Wesley today. He wants us, just the way he made us. The old times and the old men was not the secret. Their secret was the Holy Spirit. You plus the Holy Spirit — you are equally as great.'

In totally different circumstances the first American Fire Conference was held at Arlington, Texas, later in the same year. It too was greatly blessed. One delegate wrote to confirm that his son was healed of brain damage at the conference. Many lives were touched and many were fired up for Holy Spirit evangelism.

Reinhard has never been happy on a conference platform. He would always rather be fishing than talking about catching fish. But these Fire Conferences have proved to be different because of the motivating impact on the delegates of the demonstration of the power of God in action. One African brother came up to Reinhard at the end of one event and declared, 'Bonnke, sir, what you are doing is not so special. Any man can do those things.'

'Then go and do them, and God will bless you,' Reinhard replied.

That man returned home and began to preach and pray for the sick in the same New Testament style, with the power of the Holy Spirit. Today he is a fruitful evangelist in his native Nigeria.

Chapter 19

The African Trail:
Triumphs and Trials

A second trail which burst from the skyrocket of the Harare Fire Conference was the new strategy to reach the remainder of Africa. The move to the new offices in Frankfurt was completed by the end of 1986. God had led Reinhard to a perfect building only half an hour from the vital airport. He had also managed to find residential quarters next door which were converted into homes for his own family and those of the team.

Freddy was now twenty years old, and for his two teenage sisters, Gabi and Susie, this was their first time in Germany. But their lifestyle remained modest and unpretentious. There was no private jet plane, no luxury villa, and Anni found that she still had to wait two or three years for a much needed refurbishment of her kitchen. Nor did Reinhard himself acquire an allotment, that very German of traditions, despite his love of growing things. Although he is a man of wide interests he said, 'I made a decision long ago to give up everything for the sake of the gospel.'

In many ways it was wonderful for Reinhard and Anni to return to their native land, but the sacrifice of being separated for many days of the year continued to be required of them. The urgency of the task, and the travelling, seemed only to increase.

The offices were completely refurbished with the latest communications equipment, including a main-frame computer which at the time was on the cutting edge of technology. Reinhard has always appreciated good equipment, and is not afraid to use the best there is in service of the kingdom of God.

He remembered an incident a few years earlier when they needed a drilling rig for the footings of the Big Tent. After much hunting they found themselves searching among discarded mining equipment, when God spoke: 'What are doing looking for me on a scrap-heap?' He understood that God intended him to plan appropriately for the King of kings.

The strategy for the new headquarters in Frankfurt was very quickly settled and working. But it was not easy to say goodbye to men like Michael Kolisang who had worked side by side with Reinhard for eighteen years. However, Michael felt the Lord calling him back to his home country of Lesotho, and both men accepted the parting and bowed to the will of God.

For the German members of the team like Eugen Würslin who had been with the team since early days, the move was easy, but for those South Africans who had joined the team it was especially traumatic. Their South African passports were not accepted in many of the African countries which were now opening to Reinhard. For the South African team members who did move to Frankfurt, this presented them with a real problem, for they could not visit other nations until they had acquired a new nationality, a process of many years. In other cases, God miraculously intervened, enabling the bureaucracy to be overcome. Fortunately some of his key people of other nationalities were able to make the move to Frankfurt with few difficulties.

Journalist Ron Steele, the author of the two popular books about Reinhard, *Plundering Hell* and *Populating Heaven*, struggled to come to terms with the changes but finally realised that the Holy Spirit was telling him 'he had to let go'. He said, 'My almost four-year association with Reinhard and the team had been the best, most exciting and most rewarding spiritual years of my whole life.' There were many more similar testimonies from others who found there was no alternative but 'to let go'.

At first Reinhard wanted to donate the Witfield property to some Christian organisation but unfortunate differences between hopeful recipients forced him to think again. It was another painful experience for him but in the end, even though he knew that some would accuse him of 'changing his mind', he knew that he had been left with no option but to sell. The South African office was to be 'virtually wound down' with Mrs Thea Britz, the only remaining member of the local team, running things temporarily from a converted garage at the side of her home. Little did anyone know at the time that this office would flourish and even continue to contribute to the work in the rest of Africa. Reinhard may have gone to live elsewhere for the good of the ministry, but the impact that CfaN had made on many lives would never be forgotten.

Very quickly the Frankfurt strategy was made public.

First: Africa shall be saved. Africa remained the focus and priority of Christ for all Nations. Secondly: For revival in Europe. The Holy Spirit told us very clearly that our move to Frankfurt was in connection with God's plan for Europe. Thirdly: gospel campaigns in all the world. We will be active worldwide. The cross of the Lord Jesus Christ is not only in the centre of our CfaN emblem, but also in the middle of our lives and ministry.

In prayer, Reinhard found himself visualising the map of Africa, with two arrows moving gradually northwards, one on the west and one on the east, with a fine net connecting the two. The idea was to create two fully equipped teams, taking on about twelve campaigns each year, divided between them and so sharing the load. To enable this to be feasible, the duration of these campaigns had to be reduced to one week instead of the several weeks of some of the earlier events. Eventually it was settled that the West African base would be in Lagos, Nigeria, and the East African base would be in Nairobi, Kenya, with the HQ in Frankfurt.

For two years Reinhard and his team had tried in vain to get permission to hold a major campaign in Malawi, but then following the Fire Conference in Harare in 1986, they were surprised to receive an invitation from Malawi. A Malawi Government official told Reinhard, 'Do you know why we wanted you to come to Malawi? Because we heard that you had housed our Malawian preachers in the top hotel in Harare at your expense. That touched our hearts and we saw that you were not a racist.'

The campaign in Malawi in August 1986 was so successful that CfaN dubbed it 'The Malawi Miracle'. The final gathering was in the region of 150,000 and the number of responses for salvation was phenomenal. Furthermore they were invited to return in October and November for a campaign in Lilongwe, the nation's capital, and Malawi's Life-President, Dr Kamuzu Banda, signified his willingness to open the campaign.

On their return in October for the campaign in Lilongwe, Reinhard and some of his team were invited for an audience with President Banda, after which they were astonished to hear that 'Parliament was being adjourned' and Reinhard was asked if he would address the honourable Members for one hour. Needless to say, Reinhard accepted and found that the House was in full session, with all 120 Members present from every constituency in the land.

At the Harare Fire Conference the prophecy had declared that 'God's servant will stand before kings and rulers' and that 'whole nations will be saved'. Standing before the nation's Members of Parliament, Reinhard opened his Bible and preached, as he later said, a 'red-hot gospel message'. It was clear that the Holy Spirit was brooding over this august gathering and more than half of them responded to the invitation to commit their lives to Jesus Christ. The sick were then prayed for in the name of Jesus. The Speaker of the House informed Reinhard that some of the Members of Parliament had requested counselling and the Speaker offered his own office for this purpose. What a start to the campaign! The press wanted interviews with the evangelist who had been invited by the President to address Parliament, and the whole nation was impacted with the gospel. The response and the signs and wonders were tremendous.

The openness of a growing number of African nations to the gospel was most encouraging. On three occasions in three different African countries, Reinhard has had the privilege of addressing the elected representatives of the nation in their Houses of Parliament and has personally met fifteen heads of state. He said, 'While governments in the West become more cynical toward the move of God in the earth, this is not the case in Africa.' The opening up of the rest of the African continent to the team was clearly accelerated by the move to Frankfurt.

It was during a meeting in Scandinavia that year that Reinhard received the sad news that his father, Hermann, had died. He rushed back to Germany to be with his family. It was the end of an era, and Reinhard would never forget his debt of gratitude to him.

The campaigns continued through 1987 and 1988 at an increasing rate, and in the coming five years Reinhard would complete seventy major campaigns in Africa and around the world, at the rate of more than one per month. Almost without exception, once he visited a country he was asked to return again and again, but his urge was to press on and cover new ground. Cities were selected as the Spirit led, and as the political doors opened. Following the example of the apostle Paul, main population and trading centres were chosen if possible.

In 1987 he was back in Malawi for his third campaign, and twice he was in Cameroon. He was in Ho, Ghana for his eighth campaign in two years with numbers climbing all the time. In Ghana the crowds averaged between 70,000 and 80,000 and a total of 200,000 responded to the invitation to receive Christ as

Saviour. One local pastor said, 'Reinhard Bonnke's preaching is understood by the women at the market and that's why the crowds respond so well.'

John Wesley knew that, but like Reinhard he had to work hard to make it simple and to keep it simple. One of Wesley's methods was to try out his sermons on the kitchen maid. Anything she failed to understand first time he altered until she grasped his meaning immediately. Reinhard discovered equally that it is essential never to be clever but always to be clear.

In June 1988, Reinhard conducted his first campaign in Kenya, in the beautiful capital city of Nairobi. Months beforehand, CfaN's team of technicians and organisers began arriving to commence preparations. Some of them were involved in the heavy task of transporting the Big Tent from Tanzania. The campaign there in November 1987 had been cut short by government officials after only four days, when the crowds had grown to 40,000, with thousands responding to the appeal to receive Christ.

Reinhard was wrestling with a problem. Should they use the Big Tent in Nairobi? But it was more than that. He knew that the time had come when he had to make a decision about the future of the Big Tent. On his own admission, he is not what some Christians term 'a fleece' person, referring to the incident when Gideon put out a wool fleece to help him find the will of God (Judges 6:36&39). On this occasion Reinhard felt it was permissible for him to 'put out a fleece'. As he prayed he felt it right to trust that if the campaign numbers could be contained in the tent he should keep it, but if the numbers were greater he would give the tent away.

He did not want to give up the Big Tent but it was soon abundantly clear that the crowds were going to be far too big for the tent, and so it happened that the Big Tent was not pitched in Nairobi. Shortly afterwards Reinhard gave it to Peter Pretorius, an evangelist working in Mozambique, who would use it for a hospital and meeting place for evangelism. With it went many of the trucks, and even a substantial donation to help cover the costs of setting it up.

Peter van den Berg described the Big Tent as being like a rocket motor, which after a successful launching then falls back to earth, having served its purpose. Although the tent was given away, the ancillary equipment continued to be used by CfaN for their African campaigns. Events were to prove that this was another difficult but correct decision which was made at the right time. So finally one of the last umbilical cords with the past had been cut. CfaN was now a much leaner, fitter team, operating from a modern base, and able to achieve much more with much less.

As for the Nairobi, campaign its success was breathtaking. Some 211 churches from forty-five different denominations supported it. It was a wonderful demonstration of unity and in accord with the way God had been dealing with Reinhard over recent years. For many years Reinhard and Anni worked within the framework of their own denomination, and God blessed their evangelistic endeavours. But as their campaigns grew, the Lord spoke to them and gave them a burden for churches outside their own denomination. Reinhard consulted his denominational leaders and shared God's vision with them, and they were in agreement and released him for evangelism across all denominational frontiers. He says, 'Ever since I have obeyed the voice of the Spirit, we have seen abundance. I, "being sent out by the Holy Spirit", began to work in harmony with the whole body of Christ. It was like opening the sluice gates of a dam. Once we begin to calculate and protect our own little patch, the river is diverted. Insular people become isolated.'

The Nairobi campaign was held on the premier site of Uhuru Park. The first official event was a banquet with the Deputy Speaker of the National Assembly, the Hon Stephen K. Musyaka, as a guest of honour, along with many leading figures in the community. The first Sunday campaign meeting started with a crowd of 95,000 people; many responded to the salvation appeal and many were healed. The press made it their business to follow up some of the healings, and testimonies appeared in such papers as *The Standard*. All of this increased the interest and the crowds continued to grow.

News of the fact that the State President, His Excellency Daniel Arap T. Moi, had requested an audience with Reinhard was greeted with great joy even as the news came through that the President himself would attend the Thursday evening crusade meeting.

True to his word the President duly came, accompanied by the Vice-President, eight of his cabinet ministers and a number of staff. Three cabinet ministers openly responded to the appeal to receive Christ as Saviour, and the following day, three Bibles were presented to the President, with follow-up material for them. President Moi told Reinhard that he would personally give the literature to his ministers. He is a devout Christian and he and Reinhard read the Scriptures and prayed together.

The President also informed Reinhard that he had ordered the Ministry of Information and Broadcasting to broadcast the final two campaign meetings live throughout the nation on television and radio. This unique privilege had never been granted for anything other than official state occasions. The broadcasts went out for three hours on both days to the entire nation of twenty-two million people, and the radio broadcasts carried over into many of the neighbouring countries as well. Letters came in from as far as Zanzibar of hundreds of people who had received Christ as Saviour while listening in their homes. The final meeting in Uhuru Park saw some 185,000 people packed in. President Moi personally invited Reinhard and his team to return often to Kenya.

In August, Reinhard was in Nakuru for the second campaign in Kenya. Nakuru is the home of President Moi, and is world famous for the tens of thousands of flamingos that flock to Lake

President General Sani Abacha of Nigeria welcomes Reinhard Bonnke

Reinhard Bonnke with President Mathieu Kerekou of Benin

President Yahya Jemmah of The Gambia

President Daniel arap T. Moi of Kenya

Evangelist Reinhard Bonnke is well known to many African heads of state and has spoken several times to assembled houses of parliament. He has become a firm friend to many presidents and paupers alike.

President Idriss Deby of Chad

Parakou, Benin, 1996. The city's first ever major Gospel campaign.

Maroua, Cameroon, 1997. 53,000 make decisions for Christ in just six days.

Lubumbashi, D.R. Congo, 1994. A gathering of over 90,000 people in a single meeting.

Targeting the major population centres of Africa, the CfaN gospel campaign team moves from nation to nation. Cities are touched and countless lives are changed through massive open-air meetings.

AFRICA

The third 'Operation Philip' campaign was held in Mbuji-Mayi, Zaire, 1991. Twenty-five tons of equipment, including a sound system that can reach 1.6 million people, was flown across the jungles of Africa to reach deep into the heart of the continent. From a population of only 400,000, over 360,000 people gathered together in a single meeting to hear and witness the 'signs following Gospel'.

Every new believer is given a free copy of Reinhard Bonnke's book *Now that you are Saved*. Their details are carefully recorded and given to the local church for follow-up purposes.

Great rejoicing as witchcraft items are burned.

Throughout Africa, the pattern is the same; hundreds of thousands of souls are being transformed as the gospel message is preached. Signs and wonders follow; the sick are healed and people are set free from witchcraft.

The Gospel message is being preached throughout Africa. Hungry souls reach out for the Word of God and the nations are impacted with the Gospel message. The vision of a 'continent, washed in the Blood of Jesus', is becoming a reality.

Nairobi, Kenya, June 1988, Uhuru Park was the scene of a great Gospel campaign that, at the instruction of the President, Daniel arap T. Moi, was broadcast live across the nation.

Kaduna, Nigeria, October 1990. Record breaking attendance: 500,000 people in a single meeting - 25 acres of souls. A total of 1.67 million attended over the six nights of meetings.

Establishing a new benchmark for the urgency of evangelism amongst church leaders of the European nations, Euro-Fire Conferences were convened in three major centres.

Background; a part of the crowd that packed into the Belem Park, Lisbon, to hear the gospel message during the evening meetings of the Euro-Fire '90 Conference.

Euro-Fire Conference '87, Frankfurt, Germany up to 14,000 people attended each of the evening services in the Festhalle between the 5th and 9th August 1987.

Euro-Fire Conference '88, Birmingham/England. The Arena and two overflow halls were packed with close to 20,000 people.

Euro-Fire; Lisbon, Portugal. From the 22nd to 26th August 1990, crowds of 12,000 gathered for the 4th "Fire" conference.

Whilst keeping his focus on the vision of reaching the continent of Africa with the Gospel message, Reinhard Bonnke holds major campaigns in cities across the world.

Jakarta, Indonesia 1995. Crowds swell to 105,000 in a single meeting.

With a vision of 'Cape Town to Cairo', the ministry presses ever northwards through the continent of Africa. Gospel campaigns, linked together with literature distribution projects, are reaching Africa and the rest of the world with the good news.

120,000 people attend a single service in Manila, the Philippines, 1988

The Gospel will be preached in all the world ...and then the end will come. Matthew 24:14

Signs and wonders follow the preaching of the word. A Blind woman receives her sight - Jesus is the healer!

Gospel campaign in Madras, India: part of the huge crowd that came together to hear the Word of God. A total of 600,000 attended during the 6 day campaign; 150,000 pressing into the grounds on the final night.

INDIA

Up to 200,000 people come together in a single meeting as the message is proclaimed in the great cities of India. Hundreds of Churches work together in a spirit of unity to follow up the river of new decisions for Christ.

'*As for me and my house; we will serve the Lord...*'

Joshua 24:15

Jeannette, Kai-Uwe, Adrian and Alicia Bonnke

Gabriele, Annika, Christopher and Dario Navac

Brent, Susanne and Bianca Urbanowicz

Nakuru. The President again received Reinhard and his team in the State House. He also attended the opening service of the campaign and invited Reinhard to breakfast with him the following morning, where he informed Reinhard that he had ordered the entire campaign to be broadcast live on the State's Voice of Kenya network; so once again the campaign was sent out live on television and radio.

The radio broadcasts carried over into no fewer than seven of the surrounding nations in East Africa. Some amazing testimonies came back as a result. In Uganda, two Christians were jailed while entering the country to share the gospel. They had somehow managed to bring in a radio with them, which they still had with them in prison. They tuned in to the Voice of Kenya station and the whole block was able to listen to the campaign service and when Reinhard preached, the entire cell block of eighty-five men expressed their desire to receive Christ as Saviour. The two Christians were able to counsel many of them before the authorities kicked them out of the prison! From Tanzania reports came back of over 200 receiving the baptism of the Holy Spirit through the broadcast.

The population of Nakuru is only 120,000 but there were as many as 135,000 in a service. People poured into the campaign from all over the famous Rift Valley. The campaigns, linked with the broadcasts, brought the gospel to many millions, and the number of those who confessed Christ was too great to compute accurately but it must have been in the hundreds of thousands, and may even have been as many as a million. As evangelist D. L. Moody once said when asked how many had come to Christ through his preaching, 'I cannot say. I am not responsible for keeping the Lamb's book of life.' But heaven certainly keeps a perfect record and the recording angels must have been working overtime as they kept watch over Kenya during those momentous months. Without question, the whole nation was changed by these two events.

From this time the campaigns in Africa increased in frequency, size and effectiveness. Certainly the Nairobi and Nakuru campaigns marked a new level of revival power. Within a week local churches in Nakuru saw their attendance jump to 'standing room only'. One year after the Nairobi campaign they reported that 17,400 people had been baptised in water as a result of the campaign. The healings were numerous and convincing. One man aged about forty who had been deaf and dumb from birth was totally set free, speaking and hearing for the first time, his face radiant with joy. A year later, when the team returned to make a video entitled *The Fruit that Remains,* they went to this man's village, where they found that he had become an evangelist, and that his dearest possession was a transistor radio. There were many notable conversions which made a special impact, such as the repentance of an international criminal.

At the close of the Nairobi event, some of the Kenya press challenged Reinhard Bonnke: 'Why do you come to a beautiful park and preach the gospel? Why don't you go to a slum area, like Mathare Valley?'

It was Reinhard's kind of challenge, and his response was immediate, 'When I come back to Nairobi, Mathare Valley is the place where I shall go.' In February 1991, he was able to keep his word.

At first, people from outside the area were afraid to attend the campaign in this notorious location because of the many drug addicts, criminals, prostitutes and thieves known to live there. But as Reinhard lifted up 'the Christ who was the friend of publicans and sinners' they were captivated. He proved in the dens and brothels of Mathare Valley that Christ did not come to call the righteous but sinners to repentance, and the great Physician worked outstanding miracles of body and soul.

The presence of God somehow permeated the area and crime dramatically decreased. This has happened so many times now in his campaigns that Reinhard says, 'In different countries where police are very careful to make statistics, we are told that crime rates have dropped seventy-five per cent, even up to one hundred per cent sometimes, during our campaigns. Why? Because the gospel attacks these cancerous growths of sin in human society.' So far as could be ascertained there was not one case of mugging in the area during the campaign.

At the same time, the work really blossomed in western Africa. Working according to the dry seasons, which fortunately alternated from East to West Africa, the two arms of the team were now in full swing.

Nigeria was one of the most important nations, being the most populous of the continent, with over ninety million inhabitants. A great wave of successes followed the Ibadan meeting. Among others, Lagos drew crowds of 150,000; Port Harcourt, 100,000; Enugu, 140,000; Warri, 140,000; Joss, 145,000. These huge campaigns climaxed in the mighty event at Kaduna in October 1990. However, before that, the team were in for a nasty shock.

In September, the team went to Jinja for the second event in the nation of Uganda, having visited Kampala the year before. Jinja is the second city, perched on the high banks of the Nile where the river leaves Lake Victoria. It is a dusty, broken city in a beautiful setting, revealing Uganda's troubled past.

Almost from the very beginning the testimony of the gospel in Uganda had been sealed with the blood of willing martyrs. Stirred and challenged by the death of David Livingstone, Henry M. Stanley came to Uganda in 1874, subsequently calling for Christian missionaries to follow up what he had begun, and they were quickly forthcoming, but many were violently martyred. In spite of all this Christianity continued to grow. Later as a British protectorate Christianity prospered until, after gaining their independence in 1962, anarchy increased and in 1971 the notorious Idi Amin seized power. His crazed

dictatorship brutalised the country with intense persecution of
the Christians. The actual number martyred during his eight-year
rule was probably between 300,000 and 400,000.

There often seems to be a link between persecution and
revival. Other have observed that the Holy Spirit seems to
anticipate where persecution will come and prepares his people
for that by revival. Reinhard had seen it happen in Soweto years
earlier. It would happen again in cities familiar to CfaN as
venues of mighty campaigns, but which later grabbed
international headlines for tragedy and persecution.

Ugandan Bishop Festo Kivengere wrote about the time when
Amin was in power: 'Although thousands are dying for Christ,
the exciting thing is that, in spite of this, young people and old
ones are turning to the Lord during this new persecution,
challenged and drawn by the testimony and lives of those who
have died. A living church cannot be destroyed by fire or by
guns.'

When Reinhard and his team arrived at Entebbe Airport they
were given a VIP welcome. Amin was gone and the country was
struggling to rebuild, but everything promised fair for this event.
Thousands had turned out for a welcome parade with the help of
co-operative police officers. The now familiar red and black
banners and posters festooned the streets announcing the 'Great
Gospel Crusade'. Reinhard's East African co-ordinator Steve
Mutua had prepared the ground well — there was a wonderful
sense of anticipation and the churches had been brought together,
believing for a great harvest of souls.

Jinja had a population of around 70,000. During the troubles
it had become something of a city of refuge for many, with the
result that many churches in the area were new and young. The
first two nights of the event went well and there were thousands
of decisions for Christ and faith-building miracles of healing. As
team member Christine Darg reported, 'The blind received their

sight and testimonies of cured diseases created a sensation on the sports field of Jinja.'

On the third evening Reinhard was preaching on the blood of Jesus when heavily armed police stormed into the meeting and surrounded the platform. Some carried AK-47 automatic weapons. The police officer walked on to the platform and told Reinhard he must stop preaching and tell the people to leave.

Reinhard replied, 'I will not tell them,' and handing the microphone to the police officer he said, 'You must tell them.'

As the police officer took it his officious attitude changed. He told the distressed crowds apologetically and sheepishly, 'The orders are from above. It's not my decision.'

The people in the crowd shouted out in protest, 'Why? Why?' He repeated the command when the people were reluctant to move and insisted that the taking of photos and videos must stop at once. Reinhard felt that he had no alternative as a Christian but to submit to the police as representing the authority of the country. He left the stage and was driven from the grounds.

The police armed with their AK-47 rifles charged into the crowds of bewildered people forcing them to leave. Some of the police used their batons to beat them. Others of them moved into the prayer tent and began to use their sticks on the people who had come for prayer. The other team members witnessed this brutality with their own eyes. This happened in spite of the fact that CfaN had the necessary permits, all sixteen of them, from the national and local governments and was in violation of Uganda's claim to guarantee religious freedom.

Reinhard was deeply shocked. Alone in his hotel room he began to pray. As he sought the face of God he saw Calvary in a new light. Isaiah's prophetic words of the suffering Christ came to him with added meaning: 'He was despised and rejected by men ... he was despised, and we esteemed him not' (Isaiah 53:3). Reinhard's heart broke before God and he suddenly saw aspects of the glory of God that only become visible through suffering for his name's sake. The burden of Africa's by now 550 million inhabitants weighed heavily upon him. Early the next morning as he prayed he said he felt as if the whole of Africa was calling to him.

Reinhard shook the dust from his feet and flew to Nairobi. He said he would have been willing to return to continue the event but, 'The Holy Spirit told me not to trust the permit paper.' Events confirmed that he had been led accurately.

It appears that it was the District Administrator of Jinja who suddenly took it upon himself to stop the meetings, ignoring the official permits which had been granted. A phone call from Jinja revealed that even though the church organisers had received permission to continue the event from officials in the Ugandan capital of Kampala, the District Administrator was reported as saying, 'If Kampala wants to rule here, let them come and rule. But as long as I am in control here, this meeting will not continue.'

Conducting events across Africa is not always easy or glamorous. It is hard and often dangerous, but it is rewarding and Reinhard and his team will continue as long as God enables them. Even this happening in Jinja served to emphasise to the world at large the potentially dangerous plight of many Christians in some parts of Uganda. But the Ugandan church, with such a history of triumph over the most terrible persecution, will by God's grace overcome again.

During his time with the church leaders in Jinja Reinhard exhorted them, 'You must heed the words of the gospel where it says that the disciples went forth, the Lord working with them to confirm their words. You must take the initiative. You must go forth in Jesus' name, and the Lord will run to keep up with you! He will confirm with signs and wonders the words you proclaim! If there is no proclamation, there can be no confirmation.'

The Jinja campaign and the brutal intervention of the authorities only served to strengthen Reinhard's faith in the power of the Holy Spirit. Indeed, it was while he was still in Uganda, before the event was brought to its untimely halt, that God dramatically expanded Reinhard's vision of how to reach the whole of Africa for Christ.

Jinja is the place where the artery of the Nile begins its life-giving flow to the Egyptian Delta over 2,000 miles away. In September 1990, as Reinhard stood looking at it, 'the Great River' became a symbol to him of the flow of God's Spirit. He 'saw' the divine Spirit coursing like the waters of Ezekiel's vision, ever-increasing, flooding the lands of Africa, bringing fertility to entire spiritual deserts, reclaiming them for the gospel of Jesus Christ.

In the twelve months leading up to Jinja, from September 1989, in fourteen major campaigns, he had preached face to face to a total of more than five million people, and seen around one million souls coming to Christ. From the African nations of Nigeria, The Cameroon, Rwanda and Burkina Faso to nations as far from each other as Portugal and Malaysia, it had been an amazing year, and most people would have been more than satisfied. But Reinhard Bonnke has never been able to rest on his laurels. His heart still ached. He described it as 'the restlessness of the Holy Spirit' which he and the CfaN team had come to know and recognise. With hardly a pause for breath, the team flew to Kaduna, Nigeria, where the trials of Jinja would soon be forgotten. God had a great surprise for them.

Chapter 20

Africa Is Being Saved!

Weighing everything up it was nothing short of a miracle that they had even been allowed to come to Kaduna for a campaign. It confirmed the importance of always prayerfully seeking the leading and guidance of the Holy Spirit, for just three and a half years before, in 1987, Kaduna State had experienced one of the worst outbreaks of Christian persecution in recent times. It resulted in the deaths of nineteen Christians and more than a hundred churches were burned to the ground.

Once again they were experiencing first hand the confirmation of the old saying that the blood of the martyrs is the seed of the church. Reinhard was very conscious of this during the meetings and was humbled to feel that God had given him and his team the privilege of reaping a great but costly harvest. The Christ for all Nations team were told many times how remarkable it was that they had received permission to hold the event on the site, Kaduna's Muhamed Murtala Square, as many evangelists had applied over the years and been refused. Furthermore the Kaduna State Governor and many officials who had given their approval were Muslims. Clearly it was God's special timing for them to be in Kaduna.

Now on the Saturday night of the event, as Reinhard Bonnke looked out over the vast sea of faces in front of him, he was overwhelmed. He had seen some great crowds in his ministry but instinctively he knew that this was far bigger than anything he had seen before.

His mind flashed back to that moment in 1950 when as a boy of ten God had spoken so clearly to him that he must preach the gospel in Africa. Now here he was, forty years later, in October 1990, in Kaduna, Nigeria, facing a crowd which was estimated at 500,000. And God had given him the opportunity and responsibility of preaching Christ to them. To see half a million people in a single service was awesome. They covered an area of twenty-five acres. To have to present the Lord Jesus Christ so clearly that thousands would be able to respond and be saved and healed was a burden, but one he was happy to bear, and one he would not want to be without. He felt he understood why Malachi and so many others of God's servants described their message as 'the burden of the word of the Lord'.

It was at moments like this that it was reassuring to remember that God had called him to preach the gospel in Africa. And it was comforting to know that the Lord who had called him had also equipped him for this very task with the promised power of the Holy Spirit. Over the years he had arrived at a place in his understanding that Christianity is the Holy Spirit in action making the word of God happen. As he stood to preach he believed with all his heart that, if he faithfully uplifted Christ and preached the word of God, then the Holy Spirit would do his unique work — convicting, converting and confirming the word with signs following. And sure enough that day in Kaduna, the Holy Spirit did a great work as he had done every day throughout the campaign.

The responses to the salvation appeals overwhelmed the 6,000 counsellors, so that 'only' 200,000 decision cards were able to be completed! The final count of responses in Kaduna was a quarter of a million, in a city of just over one million people. A total of 1.67 million people attended over the six nights of meetings.

Miracles of healing were the topic of conversation throughout the city. It was reported, 'Like wildfire, the repetition of testimonies of the deaf, dumb, blind and crippled who were restored spread through the marketplace. The Friday night meeting in particular carried a special anointing for the healing of blindness. In fact, before the meeting, Evangelist Bonnke had said that the Holy Spirit had informed him that many blind people would be healed. Later, during the time for testimonies, so many people who had been totally blind came forward that it was difficult for any other testimonies to get through.'

Many cripples were also healed. One outstanding case occurred in the first meeting. Emmanuel Louis was a member of the church pastored by Revd E. B. Asenso, who was the campaign secretary, and who was able to confirm the miracle of healing from paralysis that Louis received after using crutches for walking since 1978. Louis testified on the platform and demonstrated his healing by running up and down the stage. Better still, throughout the event he continued to be seen walking around the city without the aid of his crutches. Such testimonies, coupled with changed lives, are the best advertisements for the gospel.

Another effective witness to the city was the trans-denominational unity of the churches in support of the event. The local chairman, Professor E.O. Adekeye, went so far as to say that every church in Kaduna participated in one way or another. This was a miracle in itself. One bishop observed that only a decade ago in Kaduna speaking in tongues was considered anathema. Now here were Pentecostal, Evangelical, Anglican and other churches working together in harmony. Pastors and the people had arrived at a place of spirituality where they could comfortably accept the workings and giftings of the Holy Spirit. The Anglican bishop opened the meetings. In a country like Nigeria, with a high percentage of Muslims, such demonstrations of Christian unity are so very important.

The planning, preparation and prayer behind a campaign of this magnitude does not just happen overnight. Revd John Darku, CfaN's West African Director, who is based in Nigeria, was the key co-ordinator. He knows how concerned Reinhard is about the follow-up of new believers. In fact during one of the

CfaN team's morning devotions in Kaduna, Reinhard's deep concern for the new believers was clear.

'We need to ask the Holy Spirit for more wisdom so that the percentage of the survival rate of responders rises,' he said. 'Just as the mother of Moses carefully sealed his basket with pitch to ensure his life at a very crucial stage, so we must be even more diligent in our follow-up methods for the new believers. Like that mother of Moses, we must do everything possible to seal their environment, to plug every hole, so that nothing of the world will seep in; otherwise our babies will drown! We don't want the next generation to miss a Moses!'

John Darku was very relieved that he could tell Reinhard how thorough the team's methods had been, ensuring what Reinhard wanted — a higher retention of new believers. For a year the co-operating pastors had been regularly instructed on the importance of follow-up visits, and about baptising and teaching the new believers how to walk in the Spirit, and the absolute necessity of regularly studying and feeding on the word of God. The decision cards were being carefully distributed to churches according to the new believer's neighbourhood. Letters were being sent out inviting them to a week of teaching on such subjects as assurance of salvation.

As in all his campaigns Reinhard made a point of meeting personally with these pastors to thank and encourage them. He poured his heart out to them and challenged them from the word of God, exhorting them, 'Don't expect Jesus to confirm in your church what you are too embarrassed to preach. It is futile to pray for revival and then expect God to step down and do what he has commanded us to do. Preaching the gospel causes revival.'

Weeks of special prayer had preceded the event, led by Suzette Hattingh and her team. As they continued to pray during the preaching, Suzette and her team felt the Holy Spirit had given them an assurance that 'God has done a deep, deep work in Kaduna. We have a great inheritance of souls here, and the fruit shall remain.'

Reflecting afterwards Reinhard confessed, 'Kaduna was awesome. God moved in a way we have never seen before. The people received Jesus in such numbers ... Those masses included a large number of Muslims, and they received the most spectacular healings from Jesus. These notable miracles fired up the momentum. On Saturday, the Holy Spirit fell on the gigantic crowd of half a million, with hundreds of thousands of people receiving the baptism of the Holy Spirit! Who can calculate the power of such a force for Jesus Christ?'

Meanwhile, Reinhard was praying about how to reach some of the more remote regions of Africa. Also, it was becoming even more urgent to be able to move rapidly through doors of opportunity when they opened.

Shortly afterwards he actually quivered under the anointing of the Holy Spirit as he shared with the CfaN team the urgency which God had put within his soul. It was the need to give even greater mobility to their campaigns by exploring the feasibility of moving the mass of their equipment by air, even to the point of using or acquiring a Hercules C-130 transport plane. They must re-containerise their thirteen tons of equipment so that it would fit into any modern airline hold. The overland method of transporting this equipment by truck is difficult and dangerous, and in some cases impossible. For example one cannot transport the equipment by truck from the north to the south of Zaire because in the rain forests there are no roads.

The team was gripped with the concept and responded with faith and determination to become 'super-mobile' with the gospel. Reinhard christened it 'Operation Philip', because Philip was the first New Testament preacher named an 'evangelist', and he was the first to 'go by air' when the Spirit of the Lord caught him away.

Operation Philip was used for the first time in August 1991, in Zaire, with the vital equipment being taken in by a giant transport aircraft. The inland city of Mbuji-Mayi with some 400,000 people is largely inaccessible by rail or road, yet 360,000 people turned out at a single meeting and every one of them had walked there because there was no public transport. Formerly noted as a centre of witchcraft, some 220,000 people received Christ as their personal Saviour.

During the period of twelve months from mid-1991 to mid-1992 it was estimated that Reinhard had preached face to face to around eight million people in Africa alone, of whom some two million had responded to the call for salvation and were directed into the church follow-up care programme, with special literature supplied. Independent calculations indicate that within the next decade, Africa will become more than fifty per cent Christian. The words of the Spirit that Reinhard had echoed throughout his ministry, 'Africa shall be saved!', now needed to be modified. Reinhard began to declare, 'I no longer say, "Africa *shall* be saved!" I say, "Africa *is* being saved!"'

Although a few governments are antagonistic, a growing number of presidents and their leading men are fully supportive; the example of such a long-serving leader as President Moi of Kenya carries a great deal of influence. In March 1990, the northerly march took Reinhard almost to the edge of the Sahara Desert with a campaign in Ouagadougou, the capital of Burkina Faso (formerly Upper Volta). This is another country which has been noted for its occultism, but twice the President brought Reinhard and his team into his home. In six meetings an aggregate of 800,000 people attended, with almost a quarter of a million people at the final service. A large percentage of them professed Jesus Christ as Saviour and Lord, including many Muslims and animists.

Then in October 1991, the team visited Kano in the far north of Nigeria. Reinhard had wanted to go there ever since the mighty success in Kaduna the year before. The Christian

Association of Nigeria had invited Reinhard to Kano with government permission to hold a gospel campaign and Fire Conference. After the CfaN team arrived however, and all preparations for both events were well advanced, some 3,000 Muslims assembled around the palace of Emir Bayero and demanded an explanation.

A senior official then promised that the Reinhard Bonnke campaign would not be held. But it was all too late and the crowd was joined at a Muslim prayer meeting by a rabble which included criminal and riotous types. Incited by rabble-rousing speeches a crowd of around 8,000 swarmed across to create mayhem in the Christian quarter of the city. In a very short time the mob was out of control and on the rampage.

Houses, shops, offices, banks, petrol garages, vehicles and churches were set alight, and Christians were butchered. *African Concord* reporter, Timothy Bonett, says on entering Kano he looked upon 'gory spectacles, corpses thrown into the gutters, corpses at the mortuaries, shops burnt and looted, cars destroyed'. According to *Times Week*, three Christians were lynched and set alight. It was a sample of the dangers which lie constantly 'just below the surface' in countries not only in Africa but across the world where some estimate that in half the world Christians face persecution. Crazed with murderous intentions, religious extremists went searching through the 'luxurious' Central Hotel where they presumed Reinhard Bonnke and his team would be staying. In fact they were elsewhere in an unassuming and very ordinary commercial guest house. This choice of accommodation, it turned out, was indeed the hand of God.

Before even a single meeting had been held, a heavily armed unit of the Nigerian Army arrived and escorted the team through wreckage-strewn and smoke-filled streets to the airport where they were to be held in 'protective custody'. Once all vehicles had arrived safely a quick head-count was taken. Recognising that a group of visiting European and American prayer-partners who were staying in another part of town had inadvertently been left behind, a member of the team insisted on accompanying the armoured vehicles back through the city to where he knew the tour group were 'holed up'. From the high vantage point of their hotel, the group had witnessed some of the terrible events of the day in the streets outside.

Unaware of exactly what was happening around them, having only just arrived from Europe the day before and having been told to stay put, they were somewhat relieved to see a familiar face. What had been planned as a once-in-a-lifetime visit to a gospel campaign in Africa would turn out to be a very short but eventful stay. The group were assembled and after a calm word of reassurance and a quiet word of prayer, they clambered aboard the military vehicles which left to edge their way through the hostile crowds outside. The disturbances had escalated and it soon became necessary for the convoy to take shelter at a police station where hundreds of locals had also sought refuge, filling the compound with a sea of frightened faces. It was only after some hours and another anxious wait that the group were to be united with the CfaN team.

Since the previous day the airfield had been closed to all air traffic and all commercial flights had been re-routed away from the troubled city. Nothing was flying, in or out, and numerous people had flocked to the airport in an attempt to flee the troubled city. For the team it was to be a long day and a night to remember. On their way back through the city, they had managed to make just one brief phone call back home to Germany to inform them of the situation. The call was received by James, the eight-year-old son of one of the team members. However he alerted the head office and soon. A world wide prayer chain was established to uplift the team in prayer. In the late afternoon just before dusk, four seats on a military aircraft were commandeered and Reinhard and an advance party were flown out. After the long hours of darkness and still under protective guard, those remaining were eventually squeezed onto the first available flights to Lagos and to safety.

Amazingly, while much damage had been done throughout the city, and the crusade ground and conference venue had been specifically targeted by the rioting crowds, no damage was done to the campaign equipment and all members of the team remained unharmed.

Despite this setback, the pressure continued without slackening pace. Each year new countries were opening their doors. Others remained firmly closed — some for political reasons, others due to civil war or unrest. Sometimes the window of opportunity is very short, such as occurred during the few months of peace in Angola in 1992. But the team slipped in for a brief campaign while the chance was there.

One of the milestones of 1992 was Bangui, in the Central African Republic, one of the poorest nations on earth. The technical feat of getting there was a miracle in itself, a journey of 4,000 miles each way. There had never been an open-air gospel event in this country, and the response was astonishing. The President received the team twice, and the people whole-heartedly received the message. Some 200,000 responded to the altar call, being a large majority of those attending.

Besides many other campaigns, 1993 saw the team allowed into Mozambique for the first time, another country formerly ravaged by civil war. Then in 1994, Reinhard reached a long-sought goal, Madagascar. This island nation is largely animist, but the Madagascans opened their hearts to the gospel, with over 150,000 responses in two campaigns.

For some time, the Spirit had been speaking to Reinhard that he would smash through the 'Ice-Cap' of Africa, those northern countries that were closed to the gospel. In 1995, the ice showed signs of cracking. Campaigns were held for the first time in Ethiopia, in Mali and in Senegal, and Reinhard had also visited and spoken in Cairo for the first time. Then in December another country opened its doors, Guinea Bissau, but it was not to be without its dangers.

In November 1995, Winfried Wentland, CfaN's technical director of their west African operations, was driving the truck with its full load of equipment, a total of 57 tons, from Mali to Guinea Bissau, a distance of 3,000 miles through some six countries. Winfried had experienced four warning dreams about the loss of the campaign equipment. Two days into the journey, the truck was loaded onto a river ferry, and the ferry sank with the truck on it. Now half out of the water, it was partially unloaded, but while it was being winched out the cable broke and the truck with Winfried inside rolled down the embankment and sank within seconds into eight metres of muddy water to the river bottom. He managed to smash the windscreen and escape, though he surfaced with cuts on his legs and body.

His escape was the most important thing, but it was surely the hand of God and quick thinking by Winfried that much of the equipment had already been rescued and was able to be taken to Guinea Bissau in time for the campaign in December.

In 1997 tragedy struck in East Africa when a land-cruiser, travelling in convoy with another Christ for all Nations vehicle en route from Zambia to Tanzania, burst a tyre. The vehicle, a recent gift to the Kenyan office from the South African office, left the road and rolled over several times. Its driver, crusade co-ordinator Stephen Muya, was tragically killed. While he sadly leaves a wife and two small children, his funeral in Mombassa was a stirring mini-campaign in its own right. Over 7,000 people gathered together to pay their last respects and to celebrate the name of Jesus — many making a first-time decision for Christ when challenged with the gospel message.

The stories of the campaigns in this decade of the 1990s must surely match those of any of the great missionary annals of the church of Christ. The message is the same, it is only the methods which have changed. The sickle has become a combine harvester to cope with the exploding population of the world.

In 1995, six African countries opened their doors to Reinhard Bonnke for the first time. In these six nations alone he preached to more than 700,000 people and over 200,000 registered their decisions for Christ. By the end of 1997, out of the forty-four countries in Africa, thirty-six had had major campaigns, most more than one, and a few as many as eight.

It was a tremendous moment when Reinhard preached in Cairo for the first time in September 1995, and hopes were high when the Egyptian Government signed a contract for the use of the Cairo Conference Centre for a Middle East Fire Conference in August 1996. However, the surge of unrest in the Middle East with the assassination of the Israeli Prime Minister and the threat this caused to the peace process, plus the slaughter of Greek tourists outside their hotel in Cairo, led to the Egyptian Government's requesting to be released from the contract.

Reinhard commented, 'To say we were disappointed is true, but this reverse can itself be reversed by prayer; and we become "more than conquerors". Jesus taught us to pray, "Your will be done on earth as it is in heaven," simply because God's will is not done on earth — except when we pray.'

Chapter 21

Good Seeds in Good Ground

From his earliest days in Africa, Reinhard realised the importance of literature in evangelism. His correspondence course in Lesotho had enlisted 50,000 students and he had even bought his own press.

But after the Harare Fire Conference in which God had highlighted the importance of multiplying his own ministry, he realised he needed to have anointed books which could impart the same burning vision that God had shared with him. He began working on *Evangelism by Fire* which was first published in 1989. It has been described as 'not being written with the hand but with the heart'. An inspiration to pastors and evangelists all over the globe, within seven years it had run to over half a million copies in multiple languages.

God was also speaking to him about 'reducing the size of the mesh of the net' so that fewer 'fish' should backslide from the truth of the gospel. He wanted a tool that he could place into the hands of the responders in the gospel campaigns so that the message may be cemented in their hearts. He therefore designed and produced a booklet entitled *Now That You Are Saved*, a powerful message of assurance to the responder that the step just taken was real, vital and life-changing. One booklet was given free of charge to each responder during the meetings, usually by the trained 'counsellors' from the churches.

These booklets were of the highest quality, far higher than many would have seen in some of the situations where the campaigns were being held. The critics complained that many respond simply in order to get a free book. 'That may be so,'

Reinhard replied, 'but we are not in the business of saving books, we are in the business of saving souls.'

This was followed by several other booklets, and in 1994 by *Mighty Manifestations*, a timely and much needed book about the gifts and power of the Holy Spirit. With this full-length book, as with many of his booklets, Reinhard worked closely with the veteran leader, evangelist and writer, Revd George Canty.

Today these booklets have been translated into dozens of languages, and it is always a challenge to ensure that sufficient quantities are available at every event in the appropriate languages. In the period between 1991 and 1997, Christ for all Nations produced a total of over twenty-two million of these books and booklets, in over 750 different editions and printings. Rob Birkbeck is CfaN's director of the international literature projects, and is largely responsible for their production and distribution. Books by the container load are shipped to CfaN campaigns from printers in over thirty-five countries. Through projects in countries as diverse as Cuba and China, Nepal and Nigeria, many are being touched by the printed word. Currently books are available in seventy languages, and his department is working on another thirty-plus languages, a notable century to have reached in seven years.

But compared with what God had planned, all this was no more than an appetiser. It had been a remarkable call from God which had led Reinhard to launch Minus to Plus. It was a tremendous task but one he felt he dare not refuse. He has been a Christian long enough to know the voice of God when he hears it.

The God-given burden was to produce a very high quality booklet which clearly presented the gospel of the Lord Jesus Christ. Starting with the whole British Isles the plan was to have it delivered to every single household, from Buckingham Palace to the humblest home. After Britain, the same plan was to be repeated in other nations across Europe, and further afield as he was led.

His heart leapt at the concept. He was an evangelist. From the crown of his head to the sole of his feet, he was committed to preaching Christ and winning souls. This concept of a special booklet encapsulating the essentials of an evangelistic gospel message excited him beyond measure. He was ready, eager to say yes.

Then, what God said next stunned him for a moment: 'I must tell you that you are not the first one I have spoken to about this, nor the second.' That was humbling and testing. Reinhard clearly understood what God was saying — that those to whom he had already spoken had not been willing. He did not resent that he was not the first. He was only ashamed that the people who had been God's first choices had been unwilling. 'Lord, you will not have to look for a fourth person. I accept the task.'

When he had first shared the plan with his own team in 1992, they could hardly believe it. 'But you are a mass evangelist.' 'There are too few of us and we are too stretched as it is. How can we take on such a thing?' 'We have no experience in this field.' 'It will cost millions.' But his faith and his boldness overrode their astonishment. With forceful determination he told the team, 'We have to have ridiculous faith.'

Even with the heaven-sent assurance of the call, it had proved a daunting task. The whole operation from start to finish took two full years of all out effort. Nothing like it had been attempted before. It was like a nation wide gospel campaign. In hindsight, it was inevitable that such a step of faith should have attracted criticism. Mistakes were certainly made, but Reinhard and his team pressed on doggedly. They had committed themselves to it and would not leave it to die. A lesser man than Reinhard Bonnke would almost certainly have abandoned Minus to Plus after some of the adverse reactions to the launch of the project in Britain in 1994.

But he knew the strategy was right. It was from the Lord. After months of work, the booklet was right — it was re-written fourteen times to ensure that it would be readily understood by every person in Britain. It was beautifully produced with a very attractive cover, and the quality print was enhanced with top quality, full colour photos and illustrations.

The distribution was planned to take place during Easter 1994, and to be completed within one week. The booklet was designed with a response card in the back, and details of all respondents were to be entered into a computer, matched to the nearest participating church by postal code, and mailed directly to that church for follow up. The responder was also to receive a second booklet free of charge entitled *The Ultimate Plus*.

The sheer technicalities of producing twenty-five million booklets was a challenge in itself. First, over a thousand tonnes of paper were needed, which had to be made to order. Then very high speed presses were required to print so many in the time available. New offices were established, a main frame computer with dozens of terminals was installed, and the operators trained to use them. The vision then had to be shared with the churches, without whom the project would fall at the first fence.

Over 15,000 churches of many denominations registered for the project, which was amazing because 1994 was the year when no fewer than three other major gospel projects were launched in the nation. These were On Fire, JIM Challenge (JIM standing for 'Jesus In Me'), and Another Look. A review of all four projects undertaken for the Evangelical Alliance was very revealing. The review said:

> For all constituencies, 'Minus to Plus' did the best informing job reaching 98% of the churches, and 78% of evangelistic organisations responded to the survey. The number of churches participating in 'Minus to Plus' was much the highest number of the four projects. 'Minus to

Plus' also had significant British Isles participation outside England.

Then the project ran into two snags — an imperfect distribution system, and an antagonistic spiritual climate. The distribution was dogged by difficulties from the beginning. At first it was proposed to send the booklet to every home in the UK and Ireland by mail. It then transpired that the Royal Mail could not guarantee delivery within the time-band of the Easter period so other carriers had to be used. These included local free newspapers, so that instead of the attractive booklet coming through the letter-box with the mail, too many booklets were almost lost among other leaflets within the folds of a cheap newspaper. In the eyes of many this devalued the booklet and according to one Baptist leader in the south of England, resulted in all too many of them being put straight into the bin, hidden inside advertising newspapers and never even seen, by the many householders who were in the habit of immediately throwing away such papers without even opening them.

Nevertheless, the delivery of twenty-five million copies of *Minus to Plus* was probably the biggest distribution of this kind ever undertaken, and though many complained that they had not received their copies, the fact remains that most households did. There were many claims that whole batches of the booklets had been deliberately dumped. Unfortunately it was difficult to prove this irrefutably, although the suspicion remains that there were those who were so bitterly opposed to the project that they would stop at nothing. Some compensation was received from distributors over failed deliveries and a further reprint followed. Every effort was made to get these out to people who complained that they had not received their copies. The final estimate was that over ninety per cent of households received booklets.

The four evangelistic projects of 1994 revealed a great deal about the spiritual state of the British nation. The exposure of the nation to the gospel on so many fronts at the same time made it all too apparent that apathy to Christianity had been replaced by open and often militant antagonism. In one village someone collected up all the literature which had been distributed by one of the projects and took it to the one known Christian resident, dumped it on his doorstep and said, 'Take these — we don't want them.'

The initial edition of *JIM Times* carried the story of a pop star who testified that his becoming a Christian had resulted in him ceasing to be a homosexual. Vigorous protests by the 'gay' lobby resulted in a print ban on the second half of the run. Civil liberty and freedom of speech had been turned insidiously into a one-way street in modern Britain. Paul Weaver of the Assemblies of God had been deeply shaken by the bitterness shown to the gospel in so many areas of the media. He said, 'The "gay" lobby, the Muslim lobby, and the media are like a corporate giant, a spiritual giant, that few ministers and not many churches are equipped to deal with.' These factors need to be taken into consideration when considering the Minus to Plus project.

However, the many millions of pounds given for these projects in a time of financial recession showed that the church in Britain, though much smaller after years of decline, still has significant numbers of committed believers who are prepared to pay and pray when given the opportunity to reach out to the lost with the gospel. There was no spirit of competition between the four projects but all genuinely seemed to rejoice in each other's success. Although there was much opposition it was by no means total and tens of thousands responded and there were many remarkable conversions. 1994 may yet prove to be the year of Britain's spiritual turning point.

Expectations had been running high. But as the Evangelical Alliance review stated, 'None of the projects matched the expectations of the participating churches. This contributed to significant disappointment. Conversion expectancy was highest for "Minus to Plus", the average church anticipating 22 responders but receiving only 0.4 (i.e. 2% of expectation).' The review summed up the situation as follows, 'It is important to recognise that in our present culture there are no easy routes to fast and numerous salvations.'

In an interview for *Alpha Magazine* (July 1994), Greg Pearce, project manager for Minus to Plus, explained, 'Our anticipation in terms of response was based on some figures we had received from the commercial world in terms of advertising and responses from unsolicited mail. Most of these figures were taken from the Royal Mail, who I think have the greatest authenticity as far as these things are concerned. We then projected ahead and thought 4% wouldn't be unreasonable. But we were also expecting a very large response in a short space of time. Clearly that hasn't happened. But what we are seeing is a lesser response on a daily basis but over a much longer period of time.'

Three weeks after the main delivery of the booklets, the daily mailbag of response forms varied in number from 200 to near 1,000 per day. After a further three weeks, six weeks after the Easter delivery of the booklets, Greg Pearce reported that there was 'no let up on the number of responses on a daily basis'.

By the spring of 1996, almost two years after the Minus to Plus delivery, the response forms were still flowing in daily. Furthermore, many testimonies had been received from churches which reported that people had been truly changed through reading *Minus to Plus* but for one reason or another had chosen not to fill in the response form. Instead they had sought out a church for themselves on their own initiative and had become part of the fellowship of the church. A half-hour documentary transmitted on Central TV Network about a year after the project included one or two such cases, and the programme was favourable to Minus to Plus.

The *Minus to Plus* booklet was a typical uncompromising message of salvation from Reinhard Bonnke. He wrote it as he preaches, expecting people to respond in a very direct and positive way. He was not looking just for enquirers but for people who were ready to make a definite commitment to Christ.

In June 1994, *Alpha Magazine* wrote, 'Two of the highest profile evangelistic projects of 1994, "JIM Challenge" and "From Minus to Plus", ushered thousands into a new found faith, and also attracted criticism and opposition.'

Reinhard Bonnke answered the critics, 'My only mistake may have been that I have expected too much. The sin would have been to expect too little. I did expect more. No evangelists are satisfied. The postal service was a very weak point. Next time we will use the official mail. We don't mind paying double the price if it will work.'

The real issue comes down to the kind of Christianity we now accept as 'the norm' in the 1990s. For example, the Koreans feel our praying is 'passive', and when the answer is not received immediately, the average Christian 'caves in' and decides it must not have been God's will in the first place. The Koreans' praying is the very opposite — it is actively persistent. Having determined the will of God over the issue in question, they will then pray and pray and pray until the answer is received.

When it comes to evangelism as envisaged by Reinhard Bonnke, there is very little difference — especially in the realm of persistence. Whether in praying or evangelistic preaching, the British give up too easily. Even if we do allow that expectations were raised too high by the advance publicity, which British church leader would not acknowledge that in general, even in the best churches, our praying and personal evangelism are far below New Testament standards, and indeed, much behind the exciting Christianity to be found in so many other nations?

A common fault today is that too many of us expect too much for too little effort. Faith alone is not enough. Reinhard says,

'Faith is not mental effort, cranked up by meditation. True faith is never faith in faith. It is faith in God. But cool and casual Christianity will do nothing. We do not strike while the iron is hot. We strike until the iron is hot!'

One of the grand features of Reinhard Bonnke's character is his persistence. Some may term it his 'stubborn steadfastness'. Either way, he just does not seem to understand what it is to give up. He frequently drives himself to the absolute limits of physical weariness, and just as often he drives his team to distraction by apparently risking all on another new venture. But he refuses to be deterred and his friends and colleagues, although they will express their feelings to him without pulling any punches, know that they could never settle for a quiet life again, having tasted life on the frontiers of faith.

Though some may doubt it, the truth is that Reinhard does listen to his critics. It is also a fact that contrary to what some may think, he is easily hurt. When during the run up to the German Minus to Plus someone publicly questioned his devotion to the Scriptures he was deeply wounded. His love for Christ and his devotion to the word of God are two of the strongest foundations of his Christian character.

His view of Minus to Plus has almost certainly changed. He now sees it as foundational evangelism. 'The gospel is planted and it is like a blessing bomb with a built-in detonator.' He says, 'We are fishing for nations in Jesus' name.' However, having learned some hard lessons after the launch of the project in Britain, he had no thoughts of abandoning it. The very opposite.

After the British Isles and twenty-five million booklets, he moved to German-speaking Europe, with more than forty million booklets, dropped in September 1995, to all the German-speaking households in Germany, Austria, Switzerland and Liechtenstein. All four countries were covered simultaneously, and more than 150 meetings were organised in these countries to present it and enrol supporting churches.

In the first five weeks, 34,000 commitment cards had been received in the new Minus to Plus office in Frankfurt. The long-term commitment to seeing this project to its completion was underlined by the purchase and setting up of a new administrative centre in Frankfurt to cope with the terrific amount of extra work involved. The funding for these projects placed colossal burdens on Reinhard's faith. But God continued to be consistently faithful, miraculously supplying all the needs. The final tally is incalculable. Even three years after the 'drop date', a steady stream of commitment cards was still coming into the office every week. The investment in terms of finance and commitment is immense but the long-term fruit is immeasurable.

Places are not chosen haphazardly. Prayer always precedes every commitment to a country. So one of the most exciting projects for 1996 was Hong Kong in November, before the handover of the former British colony to China in 1997. Over two million booklets were produced in Chinese, Japanese and English making this, most probably, Hong Kong's largest ever gospel outreach. These books were far-reaching — responses were even received from as far away as Beijing!

At the beginning of 1997, *Minus to Plus* booklets were distributed to every home in the Scandinavian countries of Norway, Denmark and Sweden, and the 1999 venture will see the biggest, and ultimately perhaps the most strategically important of them all. The aim is to cover all the 112 million households in the United States of America and Canada. To help accomplish the task Peter van den Berg and his wife Evangeline moved to take up residence in America to lay the groundwork. When completed it will mean that over 200 million households worldwide will have been given the message of the cross.

The booklet, its title, the layout and design are tailored to perfectly meet the needs of each new project and in some cases, of course, there has to be translation into other languages. It is costly, but may well prove to be one of the most vital factors in preparing for the dawn of the new millennium and the worldwide revival of Christianity. Church growth specialists are in general agreement as to the important part that small booklets and pamphlets play in preparing the ground for a coming harvest.

By the end of 1997, within just eight years, Reinhard Bonnke produced around 100 million books and booklets; each one like a spiritual explosion waiting to happen, the spark of revival in a dry land; each one good seed in good ground.

Chapter 22

The Ends of the Earth

Until the Harare Fire Conference in 1986, Reinhard's ministry outside the continent of Africa had been sporadic. Then invitations to conduct campaigns in other parts of the world multiplied and in June 1987 he conducted a very successful campaign in Singapore. Thousands were saved and healed and on the last night around 10,000 were baptised in the Holy Spirit.

But Reinhard is an evangelist with a simple message, 'Jesus saves!' And it makes no difference if he is addressing a sophisticated crowd in the West, as was revealed when he was one of the main speakers at the North American Congress on 'The Holy Spirit and World Evangelisation'. This took place in the great New Orleans Superdome in July 1987, with a crowd of some 40,000 people from thirty denominations.

Reinhard had carefully prepared his message on the topic he had been given, but when he stood to speak he abandoned his notes and launched into a traditional salvation message. *Charisma Magazine* reported, 'To virtually everyone's amazement, about one-third of those in the Superdome stood when he gave the altar call. To make certain that people understood what he said, he repeated his instructions — more people stood.' Dr Vinson Synan, the noted author and leading charismatic historian who was the chairman of the Congress said, 'I have never seen anything to compare to it in all my years of ministry.' As for Reinhard, ever the evangelist, he confessed afterwards, 'How could I presume they were all saved?'

However, Reinhard had a growing burden to reach the under-developed nations. Years earlier, on a night flight from

Singapore to Australia, the plane had flown over a massive sea of lights. He asked his neighbour what city it was, and his neighbour replied, 'Jakarta in Indonesia.' As soon as he mentioned the name, the Holy Spirit spoke clearly to Reinhard, 'You will preach in that city.' Since that time, he had been waiting for the opportunity to take the gospel to this and other needy nations.

When God led him to understand that he should 'tithe' one event each year outside the continent of Africa, he set about planning international campaigns. One of his campaign directors, Gordon Hickson, was asked to begin investigating some of the invitations which had been received. He began with a tour of the Far East, and returned with good reports from Indonesia, Malaysia and the Philippines.

The Philippines were a poor nation struggling with centuries of oppression and dead religious traditions. An event was planned there for February 1988, but ran into opposition from the beginning. The churches were hopelessly divided. Then a threatened communist take-over gave Gordon the chance to press for a national day of prayer. United against a common enemy the atmosphere in the churches changed overnight, and the event turned into a huge success. Up to 120,000 people attended, and the response to the call of salvation was often as much as seventy or eighty per cent of the crowd.

One evening two young boys approached the platform. One had been deaf, and his Christian friend had been in the prayer meetings praying earnestly for his healing. Through the prayers of this little boy, and by the grace of God, the deaf boy was totally healed. As Reinhard tested his hearing on the platform, the two friends turned and hugged each other with tears of joy for what God had done.

The following year the team moved to Malaysia, a strongly Muslim nation with a history of antagonism to the gospel. Nevertheless, God worked miracles to allow the event to take place, and once again, it was a tremendous breakthrough. Being against Malaysian law to 'convert' a native Malay, the event had to be interpreted only into Tamil and Mandarin, for there are large Indian and Chinese communities living in Kuala Lumpur. However, Reinhard preached in English, and many Malays understood the message, the Holy Spirit working in their hearts.

Then in May 1991, the word of the Lord to Reinhard was fulfilled, and the team journeyed to Jakarta, Indonesia. Another nation with a Muslim majority, Indonesia is a country of islands with a turbulent history. The island of Java is one of the most populated places on earth, and within the capital city live over seven million, with another three million nearby.

With great unity and the Indonesian flair for organisation, the local church put together a huge event, with over 100,000 filling the National Stadium. Once again, there was a tremendous response among these people hungry for the gospel. Reinhard made close friends with some of these precious brothers, and he has returned to Indonesia several times. In 1993, an event was planned for Surabaya, the second largest city, in the east of Java. Four hours before it was due to start the government cancelled all the permits, 'for security reasons'. But the pastors' conference continued, with great reward.

In 1992, with reports of revival stirring his evangelist heart, Reinhard planned his first campaign in South America. Buenos Aires, the capital of Argentina, has seen over one million come to Christ within the last ten years. This was followed by successful events in Brazil and the Caribbean.

The impetus of these international events was beginning to grow from one per year to two and even three. It became clear that, according to Acts chapter one, God was leading Reinhard to preach beyond his 'Judea' and 'Samaria', and was now taking him 'to the ends of the earth'.

There has been another exciting development in the last few years in one of the most unexpected places — India. For over 200 years this great nation has defied the efforts of many hundreds of great missionaries from William Carey to Mark Buntain of Calcutta.

Reinhard had visited India a number of times over the years, usually to visit his sister Felicitas and her husband Ron. Through that he carried out his first and unexpected Ministry there.

However, he has returned for a number of campaigns, his first major event being in Madras at the beginning of 1994. The response even managed to stagger Reinhard himself. Every night thousands openly received Christ as Saviour, and there was a crowd of 150,000 in one meeting at Marina Beach. God confirmed his word with signs and wonders, at which the pastor of the largest church in Madras, Revd D. Mohan, who was also the chairman of the organising committee, said, 'The city has been shaken by the power of God.' Of at least equal importance was the great Fire Conference which was attended by around 6,800 pastors and Christian leaders from all over India.

In February 1995, Reinhard returned to India for another outstandingly successful campaign in Hyderabad, where in five days some 340,000 people heard the gospel, and many thousands received Christ as their personal Saviour. Once again, God confirmed his word with many miracles of healing. Another Fire Conference ran concurrently with the campaign and over 6,000 pastors and leaders registered. On the last day, Reinhard personally laid his hands upon the heads of all 6,000 of these Christian ministers from across the nation — the spiritual and physical energy for such an undertaking in that hot climate is awesome.

In 1996, Reinhard was back in India for an even more successful campaign in Bangalore, which was attended by an aggregate of some 450,000 people. Bangalore is gaining a reputation as 'the Silicon Valley of Asia'. The crowds attending the campaign surpassed even those at the World Cricket Championships, which in cricket crazy India is really saying something. Some 37,000 decisions were recorded. Again, there were many outstanding healings as God confirmed his word with 'signs following'.

However, in many ways, the most remarkable miracle was that the Hindu Chief Minister of the Indian state of Karnataka was present on the closing night and he said publicly, 'We are glad to welcome Reinhard Bonnke to our city and state. There are many needs in Bangalore; I want the Revd Bonnke to pray for the healing of all the sick and relief from their problems and difficulties. On behalf of the fifty-two million of my state, I invite the Reverend Bonnke to return every year to Bangalore.' In Hindu-dominated India that was a miracle of miracles, but there was more to come.

After his speech, he turned to Reinhard who then prayed for him and began to prophesy, 'God will lead you onto even greater things.' No one had any idea what that meant, but less than three months later, by an extraordinary quirk of Indian politics, this little known man had become Prime Minister of all India.

Other milestone campaigns followed, one particular event in late 1997 was held in the central city of Pune. As is now the pattern, in each and every meeting, a clear declaration of the gospel was given by Reinhard and after the call for salvation was made for people to respond in their thousands, prayer was offered up for those who were sick. Each evening a wave of excitement was felt across the great crowd as many people began to shout and rejoice over their healing. In every meeting scores pressed forward to the platform to testify and demonstrate what God had done and the crowd roared its praise to God as each testimony was given. One such testimony came from a young woman who said that her leg had been crushed in an accident and that the shattered bone was now held together with metal screws and external braces. After prayer she was able to walk without pain. The Christ for all Nations video team went with her the next day to see her doctor and returned with an amazing report; the doctor who had taken the original x-ray photographs of her leg, could now find no evidence at all in subsequent x-rays that the leg had ever been broken! Miracles like these caused many non-local Christians to challenge their own doctrines and beliefs. Many came 'just to see', yet went home believing in 'this Jesus who changes lives'.

Alongside the evening meetings, John Fergusson, the campaign director, had organised a Fire Conference where over 4,000 pastors and workers from around the country were taught, inspired and encouraged in the work of the Lord. These meetings challenged the local pastors that they would return to their own assemblies and there too experience masses of people turning to God. Whenever he spoke, Reinhard personally exhorted them to follow the pattern of the Great Commission and preach the signs-following gospel: 'The Great Commission has its own built-in power source. The Holy Spirit is bound to honour the gospel. It burns with power. You can no more carry it out without power than carry fire without heat. The Great Commission and power are not loosely connected — they are mutually dependent. If we go, he goes. If we work, he works.'

Now with two major campaigns per year and with ongoing literature projects in India involving hundreds of thousands of books in some twenty-two languages, Reinhard, without taking his eyes off Africa even for one minute, most certainly has a heart for India. With its multitudes and diversity of peoples, the sub-continent is, as he puts it, 'my second Africa'.

Chapter 23

No Limits

Today, Reinhard and Anni's simply furnished home in Frankfurt rings with the laughter of their five young grandchildren. They are very precious to them; if you were to open Reinhard's Bible, you would not find pages of quotes from great revivalists, but the photos of these five young faces.

Remembering how his father, Hermann, had longed for his sons to enter the service of the Lord, Reinhard feels humbly thankful that his own three children are now not only committed Christians, but are actively involved in one way or another with the ministry of Christ for all Nations.

Having gained qualifications as a video engineer and cameraman, Freddy now runs the video department at the Frankfurt headquarters. Gabi married the son of a Brazilian pastor, Dario Navac, who has worked in marketing and video in the United States office of Christ for all Nations in Sacramento. And their youngest, Susie, married Brent Regis Urbanovicz, a young evangelist who until recently had run his own ministry, preaching in Africa and Central Asia. He has now joined the team full-time and assists Reinhard in campaigns around the world. Brent is a man who is anointed in his own life and has brought much drive into the ministry. He now heads up the US office and oversees the forthcoming North American 'Beyond 99? — Minus to Plus' project.

But if you were to ask Reinhard why God has gifted him with such remarkable talent to be the man he has become today, he will look you straight in the eye and tell you, 'You know I am no good at anything except preaching the gospel.'

Once you get to know him, and that is not difficult for he is the most transparent of men, you will know that that is exactly how he sees himself. He is an evangelist, and although his ministry and that of Christ for all Nations continues to expand across the world, he has never deviated from that central commitment to his God-given calling.

Nevertheless, his prowess is such that he has gathered around him just sixty or so dedicated workers, every one of whom strikes you as outstanding. Like many others of God's leaders, he seems to have that special gift of being able to discover the people with the very abilities he requires for the positions he needs to fill. Frequently they are people who have been overlooked by others, but under his touch they suddenly find their vocation in life and begin to excel. It was said of William Booth, the founder of the Salvation Army, that his leaders often came out from an interview with him 'feeling ten feet tall and ready to take on the world'.

How Reinhard sustains the spiritual, mental and physical toll he demands of himself is beyond the understanding of those of us who have had the privilege of observing him closely throughout a campaign, through a major Fire Conference, or as a speaker involving him not only in preaching but in conducting seminars and making himself available to ministers for questions and guidance. There are times when one senses that his weariness at the end of a campaign is well-nigh overwhelming, yet his ready smile is never far away and is somehow conjured up from hidden depths of strength to express appreciation to his equally exhausted colleagues.

The other side is also there. If something has gone wrong, if there has been any slackness which has caused a problem, you can be sure it will not have escaped his attention and it will be dealt with straight away! And woe betide any team member who has been careless or negligent, which might reflect adversely upon the campaign in any way, and therefore upon the testimony of Christ.

Always that is his main concern — that the cause of Christ should be advanced, and nothing must be allowed to sully that precious name of Jesus — especially in an Islamic country, or in an antagonistic land.

His team members know his standards, especially where morality is concerned. The sad moral downfall of two prominent American evangelists a few years ago really grieved him and he warned his team that if any of them were ever guilty of a similar lapse he would have to think seriously about the future of CfaN. On campaign all the team know that they are expected to conform to New Testament guidelines at all times and that means not only abstaining from evil, but from anything which might even give just an impression of the appearance of evil.

To Reinhard Bonnke the gospel is more even than life or death, it is a matter of heaven or hell, and that for eternity. 'Saved or lost?' That is the question above all questions. Others may compromise, but he will not, cannot, dare not. Yet he is not a fanatic.

When someone told him that they liked his preaching because he preached with passion, he responded that anyone can preach with passion, but unless he preached with compassion it was just a matter of empty words. He says, 'Jesus gave a new definition to the word love by going to the cross. Before the cross, love had no adequate yardstick. After the cross, the cross itself became the ultimate way by which love can be measured.'

Reinhard's faith has increased to the point where he believes that he will yet see one million souls saved in a single meeting. To have spoken like that twenty-five years ago, or even in 1984 at the opening of the Big Tent, would have seemed an impossible dream. But in the light of Nairobi and Kaduna, and the rising crescendo of his campaigns in this millennium-dawning decade of the 1990s which was hailed by many of God's anointed and discerning missiologists as 'The Decade of Harvest', it is no longer a fantasy but is rapidly ripening into reality.

It is an established fact that on the world front, Christianity is growing faster than any other religion, and much of this growth is taking place in the developing world. The twenty-first century, if the Lord wills, looks certain to bring in the most astounding responses ever seen to the gospel.

And one of the men who will be in the midst of the harvest, at the forefront of this growing army of modern evangelists, most of whom are from the developing countries, is Reinhard Bonnke. He is a phenomenon, moreover he is a German, and having dared to go against the tide of nominal, intellectual, humanistic, unbelieving Christianity, he is still pressing ahead and believing God for ever greater things. With his God, there are no limits.

Appendix

Christ for all Nations Campaigns 1975 - 1997

1975
Gaborone, Botswana
Soweto, South Africa
Cape Town, South Africa

1976
Port Elizabeth, S. Africa
Windhoek, Namibia
Manzini, Swaziland
Mbabane, Swaziland

1977
Bushbuckridge, S. Africa
Giyani, South Africa
Sibasa, South Africa
Phalaborwa, South Africa
Tzaneen, South Africa
Messina, South Africa
Louis Trichard, S. Africa

1978
Seshego, South Africa
Potgietersrus, S. Africa
Phalaborwa, South Africa
Njelele, South Africa
Green Valley, S. Africa
Qwa-Qwa, South Africa
Bloemfontein, S. Africa

1979
Pretoria, South Africa
Malamulele, S. Africa
East London, S. Africa
Mafikeng, South Africa
Flagstaff, South Africa

1980
Atteridgeville, S. Africa
Tembisa, South Africa
Harare, Zimbabwe
Bulawayo, Zimbabwe
Mutare, Zimbabwe

1981
Welkom, South Africa
Soweto, South Africa
Lusaka, Zambia
Kitwe, Zambia
Ndola, Zambia
Kabwe, Zambia
Livingstone, Zambia
Birmingham, England

1982
Newcastle, South Africa
Pietermaritzburg, S.A.
Empangeni, South Africa
Big Bend, Swaziland
Rustenburg, South Africa
Ga-Rankuwa, S. Africa
Tlhabane, South Africa
Mabopane, South Africa
Nairobi, Kenya
Ladysmith, South Africa
Cape Town, South Africa
Hammanskraal, S. Africa

1983
Perth, Western Australia
Auckland, New Zealand
Port Elizabeth, S. Africa
Dennilton, South Africa
Kwandabele, S. Africa
Tafelkop, South Africa
Siyabuswa, South Africa
Helsinki, Finland
Gaborone, Botswana
Francistown, Botswana
Durban, South Africa
Kampala, Uganda
Kwa Thema, S. Africa
Trial erection/crusade in
    the first *Big Tent*
Mamelodi, South Africa

1984
Soweto, South Africa
    Big Tent dedication
Cape Town, South Africa
    Big Tent destroyed
Calcutta, India
Harare, Zimbabwe

1985
Ibadan, Nigeria
Lusaka, Zambia
Lubumbashi, D.R.Congo
Accra, Ghana
Singapore

1986
Kumasi, Ghana
Sekondi, Ghana
Harare, Zimbabwe
    First *Fire* Conference
    & new *Big Tent*)
Blantyre, Malawi
Lagos, Nigeria

1987
Tamale, Ghana
Onitsha, Nigeria
Douala, Cameroon
Mzuzu. Malawi
Singapore
New Orleans, U.S.A.
Frankfurt, Germany
    Euro-Fire Conference
Ho, Ghana
Cape Coast, Ghana
Dar es Salaam, Tanzania
Tema, Ghana

1988
Manila, Philippines
Yaounde, Cameroon
Aba, Nigeria
Nairobi, Kenya

58 (Continued)
.rmingham, U.K.
Euro-Fire Conference
Hamburg, Germany
Nakuru, Kenya
Port Harcourt, Nigeria
Kisumu, Kenya
Accra, Ghana

1989
Mombasa, Kenya
Kumba, Cameroon
Enugu, Nigeria
Kampala, Uganda
Riga, USSR
Bukavu, Zaire
Bujumbura, Burundi
Warri, Nigeria
Jos, Nigeria
Kuala Lumpur, Malaysia
Abidjan, Ivory Coast

1990
Meru, Kenya
Machakos, Kenya
Bamenda, Cameroon
Ougadougou, B.Faso
Ibadan, Nigeria
Goma, Zaire
Kigali, Rwanda
Butembo, Zaire
Lisbon, Portugal
Euro-Fire Conference
Jinja, Uganda
Kaduna, Nigeria
Ilorin, Nigeria
Cotonou, Benin

1991
Mathare Valley, Kenya
Lome, Togo
Bouaké, Ivory Coast
Bobo Dioulasso, B.Faso
Jakarta, Indonesia
Kinshasa, Zaire
Kananga, Zaire
Mbuji-Mayi, Zaire
Kisangani, Zaire
Kano, Nigeria
Freetown, Sierra Leone

1992
Mbeya, Tanzania
Bangui, C. A. Republic
Libreville, Gabon
Port Gentil, Gabon
Eldoret, Kenya
Luanda, Angola
Birmingham, U.K.
Brazzaville, Congo
Kiev, Ukraine
Pointe-Noire, Congo
Conakry, Guinea
Buenos Aires, Argentina
Douala, Cameroon

1993
Dar es Salaam, Tanzania
Kumasi, Ghana
Surabaya, Indonesia
Tanga, Tanzania
Maputo, Mozambique
Beira, Mozambique
Odessa, Ukraine
Bamako, Mali
Kingston, Jamaica
Ouagadougou, B. Faso

1994
Kibera, Kenya
Madras, India
United Kingdom & Eire,
Minus to Plus booklet
distribution
Senajuki, Finland
Lubumbashi, Zaire
Port of Spain, Trinidad
Belo Horizonte, Brazil
Antananarivo &
Tamatave, Madagascar
N'Djamena, Chad
Porto Alegre, Brazil
Sarh, Chad

1995
Porto Novo, Benin
Awassa, Ethiopia
Hyderabad, India
Addis Abeba, Ethiopia
Likasi, Zaire
Kolwezi, Zaire

1995 (Continued)
German-speaking
Europe, *Minus to Plu*
booklet distribution
Cairo, Egypt
Dakar, Senegal
Jakarta, Indonesia
Bamako, Mali
Bissau, Guinea-Bissau

1996
Kara, Togo
Mwanza, Tanzania
Bangalore, India
Medan, Indonesia
Temirtau, Kazakstan
Karabolta, Krgyzstan
Arusha, Tanzania
Mombasa, Kenya
Surre Kundra, Gambia
Madurai, India
Hong Kong,
Minus to Plus bookle
distribution
Parakou, Benin

1997
Yaoundé, Cameroon
Colombo, Sri Lanka
Thika, Kenya
Scandinavia,
Minus to Plus bookle
distribution
Blantyre, Malawi
Lilongwe, Malawi
Ndola, Zambia
Dodoma, Tanzania
Maroua, Cameroon
Pune, India

Colin Whittaker

Colin was born in Hasingden, Lancashire, England in 1926. He was 'called up' at the age of 18 years for national service in World War II in June 1944, and served nearly four years in the Royal Army Medical Corps.

He has been a minister of the Assemblies of God in Great Britain and Ireland since 1948, pastoring churches in Rochdale, Radcliffe, Edinburgh, Bishop Auckland, Luton and Bristol. He was a member of the National Youth Council for twelve years and became its Chairman. He edited *Pentecostal Youth* magazine for seven years.

In 1978 he was elected Editor of the weekly *Redemption Tidings* magazine. 'The magazine truly prospered under the 12 years of his editorship,' writes David Pletts, Principal of the A.O.G. Bible College. He served 15 years on the Executive Council of the A.O.G., as well as being twice chosen as Chairman of the General Conference.

Colin has written articles for magazines in America, South Africa, Australia, New Zealand as well as for the Charismatic Leaders Conference for some 15 years.

He and his wife Hazel have been happily married for 46 years and support each other in ministry, especially in prayer. They have four children and five grandchildren.

For further information about the ministry of Reinhard Bonnke
or Christ for all Nations, please visit our web site on the internet
or contact the office nearest to you;

Germany	Christus für alle Nationen Postfach 600574 D-60335, Frankfurt am Main
United States of America	Christ for all Nations P.O.Box 277440 Sacramento, CA-95827
Canada	Christ for all Nations P.O.Box 25057 London, Ontario N6C 6A8
United Kingdom	Christ for all Nations 250 Coombs Road Halesowen, West Midlands B62 8AA
South Africa	Christ for all Nations P.O.Box 13010 Witfield, 1467
East Africa	Christ for all Nations P.O.Box 51121, Nairobi
West Africa	Christ for all Nations P.O.Box 10899 Ikeja, Lagos
Internet	http://www.cfan.org

Books by Reinhard Bonnke

Books by Reinhard Bonnke have now been published in over 100 languages and are available in many countries of the world. A full listing and extracts in all languages is available on the Internet (http://www.cfan.org). All titles are available from your nearest Christ for all Nations office.

Evangelism by Fire
Mighty Manifestations
Faith ... The link with God's Power
Now that you are Saved
The Secret of the Blood of Jesus
The Assurance of Salvation
The Romance of Redeeming Love
The Holy Spirit Baptism
The Lord your Healer
First of all ... Intercession
From Minus to Plus
The Ultimate Plus
Explosion of Life